THE HAMMARSKJÖLD FORUMS

Case Studies

on

The Role of Law

in the

Settlement of International Disputes

Hammarskjöld Forum, 9th, New York, May 2, 1966.

The Dominican Republic Crisis 1965

BACKGROUND PAPER AND PROCEEDINGS

of

THE NINTH HAMMARSKJÖLD FORUM

A. J. THOMAS, JR.

and

ANN VAN WYNEN THOMAS

Authors of the Working Paper

JOHN CAREY

Editor

Published for

THE ASSOCIATION OF THE BAR OF THE CITY OF NEW YORK

by

OCEANA PUBLICATIONS, INC.

DOBBS FERRY, N. Y.

1967

TABLE OF CONTENTS

PART TWO

SUMMARY OF THE FORUM PROCEEDINGS

Participants: A. J. Thomas, Jr., Adolf A. Berle, Wolfgang Friedmann, and Durward V. Sandifer

vi

THE NINTH HAMMARSKJÖLD FORUM

May 2, 1966

Participants

A. J. THOMAS, JR.
Professor of Law, Southern Methodist University

ADOLF A. BERLE
Professor of Law, Columbia University,
Formerly Assistant Secretary of State

WOLFGANG FRIEDMANN
Professor of International Law and Director of
International Legal Studies, Columbia University

DURWARD V. SANDIFER
Professor of International Relations, American University
School of International Service, and United States Member,
Inter-American Commission on Human Rights

EDITOR'S FOREWORD

The success of the ninth Hammarskjöld Forum and of those that preceded it is a tribute to Mr. Lyman M. Tondel, Jr., who conceived and has carried out the Forums as a way to fill a need identified by two senior members of The Association of the Bar of the City of New York, Messrs. James N. Rosenberg and Grenville Clark. From the first Forum, on Berlin, to the ninth, which dealt with the 1965 Dominican Republic crisis, the Forums have attempted with marked success to single out the legal aspects of problems vexing world affairs. This process enables lawyers and others to know the true extent to which the rule of law is actually working to keep the peace. Such knowledge helps avoid either excessive optimism or dark despair at the usefulness of law in controlling force. Accurate knowledge of the role of law in the search for peace makes that search more effective.

The Forum series began in 1962 with a consideration of the Berlin-German crisis, followed by discussions of United Nations action in the Congo and the Cuban Crisis. The fourth Forum, on Disarmament, took place in the spring of 1963, followed near the end of that year by a study of the International Position of Communist China. The 1964 riots in Panama formed the basis for the sixth Forum, which considered the legal issues surrounding the Panama Canal. The Supreme Court's *Sabbatino* decision was dealt with in early 1965, followed that fall by a Forum on Southeast Asia. Each of these eight Forums was the subject of a volume similar to this one on the Dominican crisis, containing the working paper and a summary of the proceedings.

The holding of the Forums and the distribution of the subsequently published volumes have been made possible by the generosity of Mr. James N. Rosenberg, the Ford and Ottinger Foundations, and other contributors. Each volume has included a useful bibliography prepared by Mr. Arthur A. Charpentier, Librarian of The Association, and his staff.

After the Dominican Forum Mr. Tondel, with his customa
modesty, quietly stepped aside to let others take a turn at running
the series. As hard as his example is to match, it gives us who
follow him an ideal to inspire us. His unfailing good humor and
generous insistence on giving credit to others are equalled only
by the high intellectual standard he set for the Forums. In them
he has built a worthy memorial to Dag Hammarskjöld.

> John Carey, Chairman
>> Special Committee on the Lawyer's
>> Role in the Search for Peace.
>> The Association of the Bar of the
>> City of New York

PART ONE

THE WORKING PAPER

The Dominican Republic Crisis 1965
Legal Aspects

A. J. THOMAS, JR. and ANN VAN WYNEN THOMAS

I. PROLOGUE

April 24, 1965—Revolution flared in the Dominican Republic and another episode in the almost incredibly tragic political and social history of that nation had commenced. As of today the Dominican Republic has a population of something over three million persons, a large percentage being of mixed Negro and Spanish blood. It is approximately the size of the State of Kentucky, occupies the eastern two-thirds of the Island of Hispaniola lying in the Caribbean almost directly between Cuba and Puerto Rico. The Republic of Haiti is sovereign over the western portion.

Columbus discovered the island in 1492. He took possession in the name of Their Catholic Majesties of Spain, Ferdinand and Isabella, and upon his departure left behind a small colony. Returning in 1493 with a group of permanent settlers, he found that the natives had massacred the Spaniards. This was the first known attempt in the New World to repel extra-continental aggression. Spanish vengeance was bloody. In the words of the Spanish priest, Bartolomé de las Casas: "This was the first injustice . . . that was committed in these Indies against the Indians, and the beginning of the shedding of blood, which has since flowed so copiously in this island."[1] The Spanish retaliation may be labelled the first reported crime against humanity in America.

The continuation of cruel practices directed against the

1

Indians, their enslavement combined with epidemics of strange diseases caused their extermination with surprising rapidity. When the Spaniards arrived there were between one and three million Indians on the island. By 1514 their number had been reduced to 14,000 and even these few were quickly to disappear. This then was the first crime of genocide in the Western Hemisphere. As the typical Spanish colonist did not come to the New World to work with his hands, Negro slaves were imported as early as 1503 to replace the dying Indians.

Columbus left his brothers, Bartholmé and Diego, in charge of the colonists, and they founded the city of Santo Domingo in 1496. But dictatorship and revolution bloomed early. In 1498, upon his third trip to the Island, Columbus found the colonists in rebellion. Under the leadership of Francisco Roldán there occured "in the name of the 'commune,' the first revolution of the people in America, this time against the dictatorship of the Columbuses."[2]

This inauspicious beginning was an evil portent of what lay ahead for Santo Domingo. Its subsequent history is a tale of Spanish neglect, bloody invasions from neighboring Haiti, years of domination, terror and misrule by Haitians, short periods of independence followed by Spanish reoccupation leading to intrigue, revolution and counter-revolution until eventually in 1865 Spain withdrew completely. Independence did not bring freedom, peace, prosperity or stability. Barbaric despotisms, continued invasions from Haiti, revolutions, political instability, poverty, corruption, national bankruptcy and chaos haunted Santo Domingo. Eventually in 1916 in order to forestall threatened European occupation and to protect its financial interests, the United States landed armed forces and placed the Dominican Republic in a state of military occupation. Eight years later, after a democratic election, the North American forces departed leaving behind some order and stability.

But this interlude was fleeting for in 1930 Rafael Trujillo seized power and became the ruthless and tyrannical dictator of the country for 31 years. It has been said that in the 473 years of its existence the Dominican nation has had only ten years of good government under intelligent and incorruptible leadership.[3]

Trujillo's reign did not go unchallenged. After World War II unsuccessful attempts were made from abroad to overthrow him. In retaliation he committed acts of indirect aggression and subversion against those neighboring governments which desired his downfall. On several occasions the Organization of American States (OAS) warned all concerned of the illegality of aiding and abetting those seeking to depose governments of neighboring states.[4]

When Castro took power in Cuba, that island became the headquarters for the training, preparation, and launching of revolutionary expeditions by political exiles aided by Cuban authorities and directed against several states. At the outset the Venezuelan Government associated itself with Cuba for the express purpose of liquidating the dictatorship of Trujillo in the Dominican Republic. With *Fidelismo* at the front, anti-yankeeism the rallying cry, and communism the directing force, an increasing and continued threat came to exist for many of the established governments of Latin America. Within the space of the first six months of 1959, several governments, including Trujillo's, appeared before the OAS officially charging acts of intervention and aggression. In each case Cuba was implicated, and in the Dominican Republic case, Venezuela was also accused of aiding the conspirators. Because the Trujillo dictatorship was so hated by many Latin Americans, there was a reluctance to take collective action to stop attempts at its overthrow; hence the OAS merely passed broad resolutions condemning foreign activities destined at undermining neighboring governments.[5]

3

No such reluctance was shown in 1960 when the Trujillo government was found guilty of an attempt to assassinate the President of Venezuela. For this act of intervention and aggression the OAS took measures authorized by the Inter-American Treaty of Reciprocal Assistance (usually called the Rio Treaty) in the form of an order calling for a collective rupture of diplomatic relations and a partial interruption of economic relations.[6] This had little effect on Trujillo who continued to cling to power until an assassin's bullet ended his life on May 30, 1961. Even then the regime did not immediately topple. But unrest, rioting, and terrorism against continuation of control by members of the Trujillo family eventually forced them to depart in November 1961. (Trujillo's successor to the presidency, Joaquin Balaguer, remained in office, reluctantly permitting the opposition to take part in the government in the form of a seven-man Council of State.)

With the ending of the Trujillo era there was no sudden resurgence of democracy. A democratic community offers privileges and rights but in turn demands service and devotion. In the Dominican Republic the powerful placed emphasis only on their privileges and rights. Hence political instability and the revolutionary habit emerged once again. Balaguer was forced out by the middle of January 1962. A military junta took power for a few days only to be forced out by a counter *coup* which restored control to the Council of State. This Council of State was able to govern although public order was difficult to maintain. General elections were held on December 20, 1962, and Juan Bosch, identified with the democratic left as candidate of the Dominican Revolutionary Party, won a clear majority. Although democratically elected on a platform of reform, development and respect for civil liberties, Bosch's term of office was to be short. Inaugurated on February 27, 1963, he was removed from office by a military *coup d'etat*

4

on September 25 of the same year. Opposition had developed from the right which accused him of surrendering to communists, and from the left which accused him of capitulating to the forces of "yankee imperialism." When he was deposed, authority was handed to a three-man civilian junta. Rebellion was to continue, however, with left-wing groups, some associated with the Castro regime in Cuba, resorting to bombing and terroristic guerrilla activities. In December 1963 an army patrol killed sixteen pro-Castro guerrillas, and in protest over this act the president of the junta resigned. The presidency was then accepted by the Foreign Minister, Donald Reid Cabral, who ruled uneasily for over a year, promising new elections in September 1965. But on April 24, 1965, the eruption which was to have hemispheric and world-wide repercussions took place.

The revolution could hardly have caused surprise. The tensions and frustrations brought on by Bosch's overthrow had never healed. Indeed, those which had emerged following the death of Trujillo still troubled the island. Added to these were growing economic difficulties. Moreover there was dissatisfaction in the army with the military reforms inaugurated by Reid Cabral, the older officers feeling that the reforms were moving too fast, the younger officers feeling they were not fast enough. Certain of the younger disgruntled military men combined with elements of Bosch's Dominican Revolutionary Party to spark the revolt, overthrowing Reid Cabral. Immediately the split in the army came to the fore and the struggle for power began. The young rebels, calling themselves Constitutionalists, demanded a return to constitutional government. The other faction, calling themselves Loyalists, sought to re-establish a junta to govern the country.

Initially the Constitutionalists seemed to be gaining victory, and they installed Rafael Molina Ureña, who had been President of the Senate during the Bosch regime, as Provisional President. But on the second day the Loyalists obtained the upper hand. At this point the Constitutionalists passed out arms to an estimated 5,000 civilians, and thousands of persons in Santo Domingo were reported in possession of gasoline bombs. On April 26 the cause of the Constitutionalist rebels appeared so hopeless that certain leaders, including the Provisional President, sought asylum in foreign embassies. But the following day the rebel assault regained momentum. By April 28 the two factions were at an approximate stage of stalemate, leaving the country without an effective government. During this dangerous power vacuum, pillage, violence, carnage, and confusion once more blanketed the nation.[7]

This then is a kaleidoscopic sketch of the unfortunate history and uniquely perplexed destiny of the Dominican people which must be remembered in any discussion of the activities of the United States and the Organization of American States in the days that followed.

II. THE ACTION OF THE UNITED STATES

Objectives of United States Action

A major target of the rebel Constitutionalist group was the police force of the capital city of Santo Domingo. Before a savage onslaught the force disintegrated, police protection broke down completely, and public order collapsed. Armed mobs roamed the streets, terrorizing the city with indiscriminate shooting, looting, and arson. It was an orthodox moment for which a handful of key communists have been trained to step in and seize power. The attempt was not long delayed. The degree of communist control is subject to dispute,[8] but it is seldom questioned that communist leaders, some indoctrinated in the arts of subversion and guerrilla warfare in Cuba, were identified among the rebel

6

forces that organized and directed the mobs in their forays and depredations.[9])

The anti-rebel military junta admitted to the authorities of the United States Embassy in Santo Domingo that it was unable to cope effectively with the threat posed by the action of the mobs and/or Constitutionalists, and consequently it could no longer guarantee the safety of the citizens of the United States or of other foreign nationals. It therefore requested the assistance of United States military personnel for this purpose.[10] On April 28, in response to this request, the President of the United States ordered the landing of 400 Marines on Dominican soil "to give protection to hundreds of Americans who [were] still in the Dominican Republic and to escort them safely back to this country." The same assistance was offered to the nationals of other states.[11]

The following day the President made the decision to reinforce the original contingent by sending in additional troops. The United States forces were rapidly augmented until a troop buildup of something in excess of 20,000 had taken place. Among the objectives for these landings were the quelling of bloodshed and the restoration of order. But the primary motive for such a large force was to prevent a communist take-over of the Dominican Republic. The United States was determined to preclude the establishment of another communist government—another Cuba—in the Western Hemisphere. Secretary of State, Dean Rusk, declared:

What began in the Dominican Republic as a democratic revolution was taken over by Communist conspirators who had been trained for and had carefully planned that operation. Had they succeeded in establishing a government, the Communist seizure of power would, in all likelihood, have been irreversible, thus frustrating the declared principles of the OAS. We acted to preserve the freedom of choice of the Dominican people until the OAS could take charge and insure that its principles were carried out.[12]

7

Objections to United States Action

There arose an immediate chorus of criticism. Some of it was based on ideological grounds for modern conflicts, whether internal or external, are in the main ideological struggles. This struggle of ideologies takes place within the borders of each state as well as among nations. Ideological affiliations have in instances become stronger than national ties, and certain supporters of an ideology feel unswervingly linked to foreign nations or groups sharing their ideological orientation, while considering their fellow countrymen of differing or opposing political philosophies as their enemies. Some criticism was based on historical grounds, the presence of the armed forces of the United States in the Dominican Republic being equated with a return to the "big stick policy" and "gunboat diplomacy" of an earlier era in United States-Latin American relations. But the most formidable array of criticism was that based on juridical grounds.

The first charge was that such actions constituted an illegal intervention in the affairs of the Dominican Republic.[13] Intervention occurs when a state or a group of states interferes, in order to impose its will, in the internal or external affairs of another nation, sovereign and independent, with which peaceful relations exist and without its consent, for the purpose of maintaining or altering the condition of things.[14] The right of independence or freedom from external political control is a right derived from the nature of the state as sovereign and carries with it the concomitant duty of non-intervention by other states. The Charter of the Organization of American States (also known as the Charter of Bogota) in Article 15 spells out the prohibition as follows:

> No State or group of States has the right to intervene, directly or indirectly, for any reason whatever, in the internal or external affairs of any other State. The foregoing principle prohibits not

8

only armed force but also any other form of interference or attempted threat against the personality of the State or against its political, economic and cultural elements.

In spite of the broad language of this provision some critics admitted that there were legal exceptions to the duty of non-intervention. Intervention can be justified as legal where the intervening state can show that its action is sanctioned by some principle of international law that takes precedence over the right of independence, for even the latter is subjected to the restrictions imposed by international law. The freedom envisaged by the right of sovereign independence is freedom from the control of other states, not freedom from the restrictions of international law which binds all states. When a state violates its obligation under international law, it is liable to encounter intervention by the state against which it has committed the delict. Thus armed intervention in the form of self-help, self-defense or to obtain redress, reparations, or conformity with legality—sanctions—is in the proper cricumstance authorized by international law.[15]

But even admitting such exceptions, traditionally international law views civil strife as a domestic issue lying beyond its province. It is considered an internal affair because on one side a people are claiming the right to govern themselves as they desire, and on the opposing side the established government is reacting against a violation of its domestic law, that is, against an illegal use of force. Being a domestic question, civil strife is in no way of and by itself an international wrong or delict.[16] Consequently there can be no legitimate grounds for foreign intervention to assist in suppressing or aiding the internal strife unless it is based on the consent of the state, and to some jurists such consent could hardly be obtained in time of serious civil strife for neither faction can speak as legal representative of the whole.[17]

Furthermore, some Latin Americans contend that intervention for the protection of lives and liberty of citizens abroad is outlawed by international law, for a state is under no responsibility to grant greater protection to foreigners than to its own citizens. Accordingly no state has a right to intervene in another state in favor of the life or liberty of its nationals.[18] Nor may it intervene for humanitarian purposes, i.e. to aid non-nationals or to prevent Dominicans from slaughtering each other, for as civil strife is an internal affair, the absence of individual protection can only be resolved by permitting the internal disruption of power to run its course.

Viewing the armed intervention as a violation of Dominican sovereignty and an intrusion into its domestic jurisdiction, it was alleged that the United States had breached Article 2 (1) of the United Nations (UN) Charter which bases that organization on the principle of sovereign equality, and Article 2 (7) which prohibits intervention by the United Nations in matters essentially within the domestic jurisdiction of a state. The latter allegation would imply that the words "United Nations" referred not only to the organization but also to each member state acting individually. It was asserted that such action also violated Article 2 (4) which requires signatories of the Charter "to refrain in their international relations from the threat or use of force against the territorial integrity or political independence of any state . . ." With respect to the American republics this provision is augmented by the Rio Treaty which obligates the parties not to resort to the threat or use of force in any manner inconsistent with its provisions or with the provisions of the UN Charter.

The use of armed force and the military occupation of the Dominican Republic was also said to be violative of Article 17 of the Charter of the OAS which declares that the territory of a state is inviolable and may not be the object, even temporarily, of military occupation or of other measures of force taken by another state, directly or indirectly, on any grounds whatever. Finally it was argued that if there were any right to intervene at all, it was not a right given to an individual nation; the only possible intervention that would be legal would be collective intervention by either the OAS or the UN.[19]

All of these contentions give rise to the vital question: were the actions of the United States legal under general or particular international law or were the critics correct in claiming that the path followed by the United States was one which was absolutely prohibited?

The Protection of Nationals of the United States

An oft-stated rule of general international law is that every state admitted to the family of nations must afford protection to the lives and liberties of aliens in conformity with civilized standards.[20] A right to intervene, to take measures of self-help, to prevent injury to a state's nationals abroad or to obtain reparation for such injuries was, under certain circumstances, declared legitimate as early as Grotius.[21] Intervention by states on behalf of their citizens for the protection of their lives, liberty or property was directed at certain Latin American nations during the nineteenth century and early part of the twentieth because the unsettled social, economic and political conditions in those countries placed aliens in jeopardy. Latin American jurists vigorously protested such interventions claiming that they violated the sovereignty and equality of states in that such action was usually taken by strong states against weaker ones.[22] It became a Latin American obsession to bind the United States by treaty to an absolute duty of non-intervention.

The United States has not considered armed measures taken for the protection of citizens as intervention. Such

11

protective action was not looked upon as an interference in the political affairs of the state. It was classified under the softer term "interposition." In 1928, for example, Charles Evans Hughes, as Secretary of State, commented:

> What are we going to do when government breaks down and American citizens are in danger of their lives? Are we to stand by and see them killed because a government, in circumstances which it cannot control and for which it may not be responsible, can no longer afford reasonable protections? . . .
>
> Now it is a principle of international law that in such a case a government is fully justified in taking action—I would call it interposition of a temporary character—for the purpose of protecting the lives and property of its nationals. I would say that it does not constitute an intervention.[23]

Some reflection of these words may be seen in the statement of Ambassador Ellsworth Bunker before The Tenth Meeting of Consultation of American Ministers of Foreign Affairs on May 1, 1965, when he announced that the dispatch of United States forces to the Dominican Republic had been undertaken for humanitarian reasons to protect the lives of United States citizens, and citizens of other countries as well, in a situation where governmental authority to enforce law and order had completely broken down. He was emphatic that this action was not contrary to the principles of self-determination and non-intervention for it was not an intervention into domestic affairs.[24]

To attempt to limit the meaning of intervention to exclude such action may not be warranted. The dispatch of forces to another nation would seem to be an arrogation of the sovereign attributes of that state and, if done without its consent, an intervention.[25] If this be true, then it would obviously fall within the terms of the broad non-intervention principle of the Americas which prohibits not only the use of armed force against a state but all other forms of interference with a state's personality, political, economic

12

or cultural elements. Nevertheless, such intervention may be legally justifiable.

In view of the prohibition of the use or threat of force against the territorial integrity of a state set forth in the UN Charter, the strong language prohibiting intervention in the Charter of the OAS, and the prohibition against military occupation of a state or the use of other measures of force against a state, also in the Charter of the OAS, it can be said that armed intervention by a state on behalf of its nationals who have suffered injury and a denial of justice at the hands of another government in order to enforce reparation, to punish and prevent future repetition, i.e. to impose sanctions in the form of reprisals, has been made illegal.[26] Hence support of legality of protection of nationals by intervention must rest on some primary right which is excluded from the non-intervention ban. *The right of self-defense* is excepted from the treaty proscriptions against the use of force and is also excepted from the otherwise absolute non-intervention doctrine of the Americas.[27] Thus if armed intervention was resorted to not to obtain redress or reparations but merely to suppress the imminent danger to citizens, to protect them against an irreparable injury, i.e. the use of self-help in a preventive, non-retributive manner, perhaps it could be classified as self-defense.

During the first days of civil strife in the Dominican Republic the situation rapidly degenerated into a state of anarchy, and there appears to be little question but that the lives and limbs of citizens of the United States were seriously endangered. In such a situation, the original limited armed intervention by the United States as a last resort to prevent imminent and irreparable injury to its nationals would be legitimate if it fell within the inherent right of self-defense.

The resort to force as an element in the right of self-

13

defense has always been recognized at general international law as a special and necessary form of self-help. Self-defense is that minimum of self-help which, even with a system of collective security based on a centralized force monopoly of the community, must be permitted. It is impossible for any system, national or international, to prevent all illegal attacks upon its subjects, and it would be irrational to expect a party subjected to an attack or imminently threatened thereby to wait for the enforcement authorities to take action.[28] Under general international law the prerequisites of legitimate self-defense were an armed attack, actual or impending, which was objectively illegal; the state exercising the right of self-defense must show a direct and immediate danger; the act of self-defense must not be excessive, going no farther than to avert or suppress the attack; and it must not be continued after the needs of defense have been met.[29]

Can a threat to the lives and liberty of citizens abroad be considered an armed attack against the state of citizenship? Traditional international law did include within the right of self-defense, the defense by a state of its nationals from violence in the territory of a foreign state where the foreign state was unable or unwilling to extend the necessary protection. A state could meet not only attacks against its territory, its armed forces, vessels or aircraft, but also against its citizens.[30] This right of self-defense was grounded upon the notion that nationals of a state are an extension of the state itself and represent a part of the state as important as its territory; that an injury to citizens is an injury to the state; and finally that an essential function of the state, indeed a reason for its being, is the protection of nationals.[31]

Nonetheless, many Latin American jurists have argued that by Latin American law set forth in codes, administrative regulations, judgments of courts, governmental prac-

14

tices and treaties, the rules of general international law have been changed so as to remove the right to protect nationals abroad from the concept of self-defense, and consequently under general international law no state can now argue that it is engaged in self-defense when it resorts to armed force to protect the lives of its citizens in another nation.[32] Brazil, some of the nations of Europe, and the United States dispute this, pointing out that neither a receiving state nor a foreigner's state can by its own law declare what is required with relation to aliens within the territory. This is established by international law. Hence when a state fails to comply with the applicable international law as regards the lives of foreigners within its territory, the state of nationality may, in extreme circumstances, exercise the right of self-defense and protect them with armed force.

But even if customary international law recognized the legality of such a use of armed force, it is now averred that because of the ramifications of the UN Charter this right is no longer in existence, for Article 2 (4) prohibits any use of force against the territorial integrity or political independence of a state. A counter argument can be made that such emergency action does not impair the territorial integrity or political independence of a state; it merely rescues nationals from a danger which the territorial state cannot or will not prevent.

A technical objection may be raised to the forceful protection of the United States nationals in the Dominican Republic on the grounds that it cannot be included within the concept of self-defense in that self-defense must be exercised against an attack that is ascribable to a *state*. The Rio Treaty specifies that the right of self-defense comes into being when there is an armed attack "by any State." In the Dominican Republic the threatened attack or actual attack took place when there was a condition of anarchy.

15

It was carried out by mobs and private individuals and could not be attributed to a state. If it is not attributable to a state, then no right of self-defense can arise. But even Ross, who accepts the point of view that when a state is unable to avert or suppress an attack on foreign nationals it incurs no international responsibility,[33] would admit that "it seems reasonable to treat all cases of attack even on the part of private individuals, according to the principle of self-defense."[34]

The technical argument can be refuted by the fact that the Rio Treaty specifically incorporates that right of self-defense "recognized by Article 51 of the Charter of the United Nations." If it is permitted under the UN Charter, it must be permitted under the Rio Treaty. Article 51 reads:

> Nothing in the present Charter shall impair the inherent right of individual or collective self-defense if an armed attack occurs against a Member of the United Nations, until the Security Council has taken the measures necessary to maintain international peace and security.

No distinction is made between an armed attack by individuals or an armed attack by a state; apparently the exercise of the inherent right of self-defense would be permitted against both.[35]

General international law permitted the exercise of the right of self-defense not only in the face of actual attack but also against a *threatened* attack when the danger was imminent.[36] It has been maintained that Article 51 eliminates this latter right because it speaks only of the right of self-defense "if an armed attack occurs." With reference to United States action in the Dominican Republic, although some few citizens had been fired upon, for the most part they were simply being threatened by imminent danger caused by the violence of rioting mobs. As Under Secretary of State for Economic Affairs, Thomas Mann, stated, "We

16

did not consider it necessary to wait until innocent civilians had been killed in order to prove to the most skeptical that lives were in danger."[37] This is an admission that the action was taken against an imminent attack rather than an actual attack. As well known an authority on the UN Charter as Hans Kelsen is of the view that the right of self-defense is now limited to action *after* an armed attack has occurred.[38] Regardless of the limitation of the clause "if an armed attack occurs," it can be maintained that when the Charter speaks of the right of self-defense as being an "inherent" right, it implies that it is inalienable, incapable of being surrendered in whole or in part. If it is truly inherent, the right of self-defense can then still be applied wherever it was permitted under general international law, not only against actual attack but also against a threatened attack when the danger is imminent.[39]

Under Article 51 the inherent right of self-defense is permitted until the Security Council has taken "the measures necessary to maintain international peace and security." Obviously, if an armed attack occurs, international peace and security cannot be *maintained*. It has been broken, so it can only be restored. A possible interpretation of this statement may be that the Charter obliquely recognizes that self-defense can come into play when the danger of a threatened attack is imminent and at such time the Security Council has the responsibility to *maintain* international peace; or the phrase "armed attack" must cover an *imminent* armed attack in the face of which it might be possible for the Security Council to maintain peace.[40]

It has been rationalized that Article 51 is merely a declaratory article designed to preserve the right of self-defense, not to limit it, and consequently contains no additional obligations. From a practical approach it has been pointed out that the political necessities of modern international life force an acceptance of the general international law right of self-defense for to limit such a right to be exercised only against an armed attack by a state, particularly in the absence of a truly effective collective security system, could well circumscribe the legal right of a state to protect itself against its own, or in the Dominican instance its own citizens', destruction.[41]

Finally such a right of defense of nationals abroad is subjected to criticism because it is so open to abuse. It may be a disguise for the advancement of nationalistic or ideological coercive designs against the state to which the action is directed.[42] Dangerous potentialities for arbitrary action are present since the intervening state by this method of self-help is judge and jury in its own case. A rejoinder can be made that the use of force in this type of self-defense is legitimate only in case of absolute need to protect human life. If such need exists, the right must be considered justified, for possible action, taken at a later time, by an international organization cannot remedy the injury where death or maiming has occured.[43] In view of the stress placed on human rights by the UN Charter and the Charter of the OAS, and in view of the fact that the right of life is most fundamental, it may be inferred that the preservation of human life must take precedence over the right of a nation not to have troops landed on its territory. Furthermore, although the first decision as to the legality of the action in self-defense must rest with the state taking this action, later review by a higher authority such as the Security Council, the General Assembly, or the Meeting of Consultation of Ministers of Foreign Affairs can either affirm or deny the legality of the original decision on the recourse to the use of force.

Humanitarian Intervention

The United States landed armed forces in the Dominican

18

Republic not only to protect its own nationals but also to protect the nationals of other countries including innocent citizens of the Dominican Republic.[44] Can the use of armed force by a state directed against another state on behalf of non-nationals be brought within the concept of self-defense and thereby be legitimate under existing international treaty bans on armed intervention? Here the connecting link of nationality has disappeared. While defense of its nationals can be considered defense of the state itself, defense of foreign nationals falls outside the realm of self-protection. Would this then negate the legality of an intervention by a state to afford protection to persons who are not its own nationals?

At traditional international law humanitarian intervention was asserted and acted upon. It was held that when a state, although acting within its rights of sovereignty, so violated the rights of humanity beyond all limits of reason and justice, whether the violations applied to its own nationals or the nationals of other nations, a right to intervene by members of the family of nations was lawful. Notwithstanding the fact that such intervention impinged upon state independence, the right of independence gave way when it was abused. That is, in international law there are no perfect rights, no absolute rights. All rights must be exercised prudently with ordinary precautions without abusing them or exceeding their equitable limits. When a state abuses its right of sovereignty by permitting within its territory the treatment of its own nationals or foreigners in a manner violative of all universal standards of humanity, any nation may step in and exercise the right of humanitarian intervention.[45]

Customary international law also recognized that humanitarian intervention was permissible in certain cases of civil strife, but, to prevent overhasty action, it was generally said that the act of intervention could take place only after a protracted civil struggle had given way to anarchy so as to create a clearly evident circumstance of break-down in the preservation of the basic guarantees of humanity.[46] If the customary rule still governs, it would seem that the need for protracted struggle would not necessarily be vital, for if actual conditions of anarchy exist which imperil a large number of innocent persons, the right of humanitarian intervention should not be denied.

A plea can be made that where it is legal to intervene to protect one's own nationals, it is an extension of this legality to protect the nationals of others. The so-called principle of nationality is not inflexible, as can be seen in various arbitral cases on the exercise of the right of protection in relation to interests in corporate bodies. It has been held that where a state intervenes to protect a corporation whose majority shares are held by nationals, it may also intervene on behalf of the foreign minority interest on the grounds that failure to do so might cause multiple interventions or might seriously injure the minority rights.[47] If it is legitimate to intervene for *property* rights of non-nationals, it certainly can be argued that intervention for *human* rights of non-nationals is even more important.

In spite of a recognition of a right of humanitarian intervention by customary international law, strict principles of modern multilateral treaty law may have completely abolished the right. The UN Charter ban on the threat or use of force could include landing of troops for humanitarian purposes. The treaties of the OAS are even more strict, banning intervention, directly or indirectly for any reason whatever.

The absolutist view that these instruments abolish humanitarian intervention has not been accepted by the United States as can be seen from the fact that it joined with Belgium in November 1964 to intervene in civil strife in the Congo to rescue hostages who were citizens of at

20

least eighteen foreign countries and who were being held and subjected to inhuman treatment by rebel forces. In addition to the legal justification of self-defense, i.e. the responsibility of the United States and Belgium to protect the lives of their own nationals, certain other grounds of legality were set forth which were also applicable in the Dominican affair: humanitarian intervention to protect the right of legation; humanitarian intervention to save the lives of innocent non-nationals; the request of the established government of the Congo to aid in the rescue; and the inability of international organization to take action.[48]

In the Congo some of the prisoners were diplomatic officials. Intervention for the protection of the right of legation was considered legal under customary international law. The protection of legation is older than international law itself, for even in antiquity representatives of other sovereigns were thought to be sacrosanct. Their mistreatment was a legitimate cause for war. Without the protection of legation, the international community would cease to function. For this reason any nation was permitted to come to the aid of another whose legation was illegally violated.[49] In Santo Domingo, among other activities of the rioters, the Embassy of El Salvador was sacked and burned, and the embassies of other nations were seriously threatened.[50] If the ancient right of protection of legation is still an acceptable part of the law of nations, humanitarian intervention for this purpose would be an exception to the strict prohibitions against the use of force in the UN Charter and the treaties of the OAS.

There are certain jurists who would defend the right of humanitarian intervention as an unwritten exception to all rules, whether set forth by customary international law or by particular international law, which ban forceful intervention in the affairs of a state for, it is said:

21

Some rights are not created by States for the benefit of their nationals or of foreigners; namely, the right to life, the right to liberty and the right to own property. The community has simply recognized the existence of these rights and States have mutually undertaken to ensure the possibility of enjoying them. . . . In fact, wherever a man goes he takes his rights with him, and wherever he is *it is the will of all States* that these rights shall be safeguarded. Before these rights, nationality sinks into the background, because they belong to the man as a human being, and are not, accordingly, subordinate to the will of the State.[51]

Other jurists would oppose this view, pointing out that in the twentieth century many nations recognize terror as a legitimate method of government, and not even the most revolting violations of the common laws of decency and humanity committed by a government against its own people or against foreigners who are not nationals of a protesting state would be sufficient legal justification for unilateral humanitarian intervention in face of the strict international contractual bans against all interventions. If nations had wished to exclude humanitarian interventions from these prohibitions they would have done so expressly.[52]

When consent is given by a state to foreign action of an interventionary character, in reality there is no intervention.[53] Unlike the Congo, there was no invitation or authorization for humanitarian action by an established government in the Dominican Republic. The established government had been deposed. Certain military and police forces of the country did request aid in the face of total degeneration of law and order. But whether they could speak for the state in face of such an emergency is controvertible. Practically speaking, in time of anarchy no one group can speak for the whole nation. It can then be argued that a request by any faction for humanitarian intervention would constitute a legitimate request. Conversely, when there is no government which represents the whole nation, only

22

if all fighting factions request humanitarian intervention can it be justified on the basis of consent.

Because of the political ramifications, in both the *Congo Case* and the *Dominican Republic Case,* it is doubtful whether the appropriate international organization could have acted with proper speed to save lives. But even if speed were possible some argument can be made that it would have been illegal for them to do so. Neither the UN Charter nor the OAS Charter establishes any right of collective action in cases where humanitarian intervention might be warranted. Under a strict construction of its Charter, the UN can only act when there is a threat to the peace, breach of the peace, or act of aggression,[54] and pure humanitarian intervention would not seem to fall within these stipulations. The OAS Charter specifically forbids intervention by the OAS, as well as by individual members, except in self-defense or in accord with existing treaties. This portion of the non-intervention principle is a troublesome impediment to collective humanitarian intervention.

It might be alleged that as one of the purposes of the UN is the achievement of "international cooperation in solving international problems of an . . . humanitarian character"[55] this would be broad enough to permit a collective right of humanitarian intervention on the assumption that the customary law right of humanitarian intervention has now been collectivized. As far as the OAS is concerned, although its treaties are couched in terms of absolute non-intervention, still it is set forth that a member state must conduct itself in accordance with the principles of the OAS included within which is a recognition of the fundamental rights of the individual. When this principle becomes incompatible with a blanket proscription against intervention, it should be permitted to take precedence over non-intervention, particularly if a government through anarchy or otherwise is unable to maintain at least the most elementary and basic rights of humanity.

Prevention of the Forcible Seizure of Power by Communists

The armed action to evacuate citizens of the United States and other foreign nationals may be grounded on an initial right of self-defense. But there are limitations of proportionality for a legal exercise of this right. Unquestionably the United States involvement in the Dominican Republic went beyond these limitations for there was a massive invasion far in excess of the troops needed to evacuate nationals. At the time the decision was made to augment the forces originally landed, the United States authorities had become convinced from the evidence that communist elements "had captured the revolution according to plan and the danger of a Communist takeover was established beyond question."[56] The continued and enlarged military presence was said to be necessary "in view of the clear and present danger of the forcible seizure of power by the Communists."[57]

That United States action which had been predicated on protection of human life was not subject to extreme criticism, but vehement protest was registered at what was called an arrogant assumption by the United States of power to intervene unilaterally in an internal revolutionary situation in a nation of the Western Hemisphere when the United States unilaterally determined that a dangerous degree of communist participation was involved. Despite United States insistence upon the imminent communist peril in the Dominican Republic which necessitated continuing action, skepticism has been voiced as to the degree of communist influence in the rebel movement and the view has been expressed that the United States exaggerated the danger.[58]

24

In any event, some statesmen and jurists would condemn any intervention no matter how great the peril of a communist takeover. As would be expected, the Soviet Union regarded the presence of the United States forces in the Dominican Republic as a punitive military action to suppress a "war of national liberation."[59] Others condemned it as an unjustified unilateral intervention in a situation of civil strife, a matter essentially within the domestic jurisdiction of a state.[60]

Under the basic right of internal and external self-determination, a state is free to choose any form of governmental political institutions it desires, subject to no interference from other states. Any intervention to hinder or prevent a state from exercising its right to choose its own government, even by means of violent revolution, is an illicit act.[61] In the Dominican Republic the United States disclaimed any intention of imposing a political solution by aiding either faction.[62] Its intervention actually prevented one or the other faction from acquisition of control of the government. In this manner it did interfere in a revolutionary situation which affected the outcome of violence and the right of internal self-determination by violent means. If this was a purely internal revolution, the United States intervention was illegal. But it was emphasized that more was present in the Dominican Republic, that the civil strife was no longer an internal matter but had in effect become internationalized. The state harrassed by civil rebellion was at the same time subjected to a degree of subversive intervention and indirect aggression by another nation or nations seeking to impose a foreign ideology —communism—upon the people of the Dominican Republic. If this were true, would a unilateral intervention by the United States to prevent the success of such externally directed subversion be legitimate?

Despite the fact that a state's action in instigating, aiding, abetting or formenting subversive or revolutionary movements in another state is a violaion of international law and has been labeled indirect aggression as well as external intervention;[63] despite the acknowledged recognition of the interventionist character of communism which has assumed the right to subvert any government in what it ascribes to be "wars of national liberation," that is "liberating" independent nations into communism;[64] despite the condemnation by American nations of Marxism-Leninism as incompatible with principles of the inter-American system;[65] despite many resolutions recognizing that the democratic institutions of the Americas are in danger from the increased intensity of the subversive offensive of communist governments;[66] and despite OAS acknowledgment that a nation dominated by the international communist movement loses both its external and internal self-determination;[67] certain publicists and jurists have continued to insist upon the priority of non-intervention and to deny a right to intervene to prevent an American republic, in imminent danger from communist activities, from succumbing to and falling within communism's orbit. Non-intervention is paramount and absolute, and the intervention in the Dominican Republic was an illegal breach of the Charter of the OAS.

This wholesale condemnation of all interventions may be too broad. A contrary position can be outlined under basic legal theory or under present day international and inter-American law. A fundamental principle in the interpretation of all law is that a legal rule can never be explained in terms of itself or without reference to its purpose. The non-intervention ban in the Americas was not adopted merely as a verbal exercise; its purpose was to protect the freedom of a people to govern themselves democratically without outside interference. Insistence on absolute non-intervention when it would defeat the very ideals the rule sought to protect, namely the liberty and self-determination of a people, would be a misuse of law. As the purpose of the rule is more important than the literal words of the rule, action taken to prevent a defeat of that purpose cannot be said to be prohibited by its bald words. Once the communists control a government, liberty and self-determination are no longer possible. For those who follow this train of reasoning, the landing of additional troops by the United States was seen in effect as an attempt to preserve for the Dominican people the right to choose their own form of government and came within the purpose of the rule on non-intervention.

A plea can also be made that the United States was merely acting under the right of collective self-defense as permitted by Article 51 of the UN Charter and Article 3 of the Rio Treaty which declares that an armed attack by any state against an American state constitutes an attack against all the American states and each undertakes to attack or possibly an impending imminent armed attack right of individual and collective self-defense. But can the communist domination of a situation of civil strife be considered an armed attack?

The Rio Treaty when it speaks of an armed attack may be interpreted as meaning an actual, illegal, direct armed assist in meeting the attack in the exercise of its inherent where the necessity for self-defense is instant, overwhelming, leaving no choice of means or no moment of deliberation. The force which should comprise "armed attack" has been broadly defined as "any elements at the disposal of states which are capable of destroying life and property or inflicting serious damage."[68] This would include not only a direct use of force whereby a state operates through regular military units, but also an indirect use of force whereby a state operates through irregular groups or terrorists who are citizens but political dissidents of the victim

27

nation. The inter-American system has characterized such indirect use of force as internal aggression in that it includes the aiding or influencing by another government of hostile and illegal conduct against the established political order or government of another country.[69] Since it is usually an attack against the internal order through an attempt to overthrow or harass the victim government by promoting civil strife and internal upheaval or, once civil strife has commenced, by an attempt to take over the leadership of those in rebellion, it is a vicarious armed attack. Thus it has been said that a government which gives military aid to groups which commit armed subversive or terrorist activities against another state by financing, organizing, training, or supplying them with arms or material, vicariously engages in the illegal use of force and this is an aggression which is attributable to the aggressor state.[70] It is a violation of Article 2 (4) of the UN Charter in that such actions are taken against the political independence of the victim state; it is also an invasion of another state's essential rights so as to endanger its security and hence its territorial integrity. The victim state may exercise its right of individual self-defense against the aggressor state, and, of course, may act against the subversive groups within the country.

That such vicarious, indirect armed aggressions fall within the term "armed attack" as used in Article 51 of the UN Charter has been asserted on several occasions. In the *Greek Case,* which came before the UN in December 1946, the United States took the position that Yugoslavian, Albanian, and Bulgarian assistance to guerrilla forces fighting against the Greek Government in civil strife in that country amounted to armed attack making Article 51 applicable:

No intelligent person in possession of the facts can fail to recognize here the use of force, however devious the subterfuge may be . . . Yugoslavia, Bulgaria and Albania, in supporting guerrillas

28

in Northern Greece, have been using force against the territorial integrity and political independence of Greece.[71]

In 1958 the Lebanese Delegate, speaking before the Security Council, defended his nation's right to protect itself against the indirect violence and subversive intervention of the United Arab Republic by noting that Article 51 was not limited to direct attack only but spoke in terms of "armed attack" which could include indirect attack. He queried:

> Is there any difference from the point of view of the effects between direct armed attack or indirect armed attack if both of them are armed and if both of them are designed to menace the independence of the country?[72]

Secretary of State Dulles, in commenting on the same issue, was of the opinion that the words "armed attack" included armed internal revolution which was fomented from abroad and aided and assisted from abroad.[73] France, under its inherent right of self-defense, in 1958 bombed a point in Tunisia which was being used for the training of recruits and the supplying of arms for use by Algerian rebels.[74] In a report on the North Atlantic Treaty in 1949, the United States Senate Committee on Foreign Relations expressed the belief that:

> Obviously, purely internal disorders or revolutions would not be considered "armed attacks" . . . However, if a revolution were aided and abetted by an outside power, such assistance might possibly be considered as armed attack.[75]

And at the Ninth Meeting of Consultation of American Ministers of Foreign Affairs, convoked to discuss Venezuelan charges that the communist Government of Cuba was training Venezuelans in modern techniques of subversion, was remitting funds to maintain and increase subversive activities in Venezuela, was providing arms to guerrillas, and was conducting a hostile propaganda campaign against the Venezuelan Government designed to incite rebellion

29

and revolution, the truth of Venezuela's allegations was investigated and affirmed. The Meeting declared that the acts verified constituted an aggression and an intervention on the part of the Government of Cuba in the affairs of Venezuela.[76]

In the light of these precedents it would seem that if communists had successfully infiltrated the rebellion, their activities could be considered an armed attack against the territorial inviolability, the sovereignty, and the political independence of the Dominican Republic. As Professor Adolph A. Berle has remarked, the situation in such a case is no longer an indigenous revolutionary movement, but an "overseas attack" on an American republic.[77]

The United States authorities viewed the threat of a communist domination of the Dominican Republic as real and imminent because of the increasing control of the rebel forces by a hard core of disciplined communists trained in Cuba. Although all of the evidence has not been made public, it was noted that the facts possessed concerning such communist influence "would fill a volume":

> All those in our government who had access to official information were convinced that the landing of additional troops was necessary in view of the clear and present danger of the forcible seizure of power by the Communists. The evidence we have indicates that at that stage the paramilitary forces under the control of known Communists exceeded in military strength the forces controlled by the non-Communist elements within the rebel movement. Equally important is the fact that these non-Communist elements were working hand-in-glove with the Communists.
>
> The strength of the Communist component of the rebel side must be measured not only by its men and arms and its superior discipline but by the weakness, the divisions and the lack of leadership within the rebel movement. It needs to be measured in the light of the fact that the Communists were operating in a total political vacuum during the early days of the crisis.[78]

Furthermore, the Special Consultative Committee on Security, an autonomous agency of the OAS consisting of

experts whose duty it is to maintain a hemispheric vigilance
for the purpose of warning the Council concerning acts
of aggression or subversion, after a study of the Dominican
situation, asserted:

> The events that began last April in the Dominican Republic
> gave rise to a typical case in which the communists attempted to
> take advantage of an irregular internal situation in order to seize
> power. This maneuver was not successful owing to the adoption of
> extra-territorial measures—well known to the public—which were
> a timely factor in preventing a greater initial propagation of com-
> munism.
>
> Later, *by means of a well-directed foreign plan,* the communists
> took advantage of a series of circumstances such as:
>
>> The privileged situation of the so-called "constitutionalist
>> zone" in the Dominican capital;
>> The well-meaning action of international organizations in
>> applying conciliatory measures; and
>> The democratic opinion of the Americas which favored the
>> principle of nonintervention. (Italics added) [79]

Hereby an agency of the OAS also affirmed the communist
involvement in the Dominican affair and acknowledged
that it was being directed from abroad.

When a foreign state is participating in internal strife,
whether directly or vicariously, the nation subject to such
attack may exercise the right of self-defense, and other
nations tied to it by treaty may come to its aid in the
exercise of collective self-defense. At the Eighth Meeting
of Consultation of American Ministers of Foreign Affairs
it was determined that communist acts of subversion would
bring into force the right of individual and collective self-
defense, for this meeting resolved:

> To urge the member States to take those steps they may consider
> appropriate for their individual or collective self-defense . . . to
> counteract threats or acts of aggression, subversion or other dangers
> to peace and security resulting from the continued intervention in
> this hemisphere of Sino-Soviet powers.[80]

Or, as the Ninth Meeting of Foreign Ministers resolved in

the *Venezuelan-Cuban Case* of 1963-64 after Cuba had been found guilty of attempting to subvert Venezuelan institutions through terrorism, sabotage, guerrilla warfare, and hostile propaganda:

To warn the Government of Cuba that if it should persist in carrying out acts that possess characteristics of aggression and intervention against one or more of the member States of the Organization, the member States shall preserve their essential rights as sovereign States by the use of self-defense in either individual or collective form, which could go so far as a resort to armed force . . .[81]

Moreover, Artcile 3 of the Rio Treaty observes that an armed attack against an American state is an attack against all the American states and imposes upon each nation an obligtion, under certain conditions, to take measures to assist the injured party in the exercise of the inherent right of collective self-defense. This obligation of collective self-defense comes into being in two stages. When an armed attack is launched within the territory of an American state, the contracting parties have not only a right but also a duty to take measures to assist the injured party in meeting the attack upon a request for aid by the victim state. The requirement that aid must be requested by the attacked party was included in the treaty to prevent possible simulated aggression which might occur under the guise of conferring aid upon a victim of a supposed attack. The second stage of collective self-defense begins with the convening of the Organ of Consultation which is enjoined to meet without delay to examine the immediate measures of assistance which have been taken by the individual states and to agree upon collective measures to be taken.

If it is accepted that there was an armed attack within the territory of an American state, aided and abetted from abroad, and if it is accepted that there was a pressing clear and present danger of seizure of power in the Dominican Republic by the communists, a forceful intervention to prevent such aggression from bearing fruit would come within the terms of Article 3 of the Rio Treaty if there had been a request for aid from an established government. Although Article 51 of the UN Charter is silent concerning the necessity of a request for aid by the attacked state as a precondition of an exercise of collective self-defense, it has been maintained that an explicit request is requisite even when there is a long-standing mutual defense treaty.[82] The difficulty in the Dominican crisis centers around the problem of who had the capacity to speak for the state and request aid? The entity normally would be the *de jure* government, but that government had succumbed to the revolution on its second day with President Reid Cabral resigning and going into hiding. The rebel-installed provisional president had abandoned his office and taken asylum in a Latin American embassy, and from April 27 until May 3, when Colonel Francisco Caamaño Deño formed his regime, there was no identifiable leadership of the rebel faction. The Loyaltists had, on April 28, formed a three-man military junta to govern the country, and it was this authority that had admitted that a situation of anarchy existed and had requested United States armed intervention. The late Ambassador Adlai Stevenson spoke of this group as "the only apparent responsible authority in Santo Domingo," and stated that such authority had requested "the United States to send in armed forces."[83] Whether either the military junta or the rebel faction could speak for the Dominican state is, however, problematical. The fact that there was no request by an incumbent government which truly represented the nation seems to contravene Article 3 of the Rio Treaty.

Still it may be adduced that the Article 3 requirement of a request by the victim never took into account nor contemplated a situation of anarchy where there was a complete collapse of all governmental processes. Accordingly, a request should be considered sufficient if, in the words of Ambassador Stevenson, it came from the "only apparent responsible authority" left in the country. In any event, a further difficulty is encountered here for although the junta requested the landing of United States forces to restore law and order and to save lives, apparently it did not request additional troops to avert communist aggression.[84]

A reading of Article 3 demonstrates that each state is expected to defend itself from an alleged armed attack for each of the contracting parties undertakes "to assist in" meeting such attack. If anarchy prevents a state from countering an attack against its territorial integrity and political independence caused by communist subversion, would other members be precluded from exercising a right of collective self-defense to aid the victim simply because of failure to obtain a request for such assistance? If collective self-defense can be interpreted to mean that two or more nations can take collective action in the right of self-defense when each state has an individual right of self-defense, then a request from the state actually under attack would not appear requisite. Following this line of thought, a neighboring state might act in self-defense if it could show some legal interest of its own being invaded. Ordinarily if one state is subjected to an illegal armed attack by a second state, this would not be an invasion of the legal rights of a third state. However it has been recognized that a third state may act in self-defense to assist another state in repelling an aggression when there exists a close relationship between the two states based on solidarity for the legal interests of both states would be violated by an armed attack against either one of them.[85] If the security of a group of states, such as those who are members of the OAS, is dependent in fact upon the security of each and every one of them, a violation of the rights of any member of the group would be a violation of the

34

rights of all, permitting joint efforts for protection. Since the OAS Charter is based on the close integration and solidarity of the American republics and recognizes the right of collective self-defense, it incorporates the concept that each state of the Americas has a legal right in the security of all other states: an aggression against one is an aggression against all. This being so, it can be reasoned that the communist armed attack in the Dominican Republican was also an aggression against each nation of the hemisphere, including the United States, and, as the latter suffered a violation of its own legal rights, it could exercise its right of collective self-defense to protect not only against injury to itself but also against injury to the Dominican Republic with no request from the latter.

Finally, perhaps the United States action could be justified on the plea of necessity which a few jurists declare is valid in international law.[86] Under a plea of necessity a state may claim and obtain an extraordinary and exceptional right to disregard the normal duty imposed upon it by a rule of international law. Necessity may excuse the non-observance of international obligations; if the excuse is valid, it excludes international responsibility. Necessity does not give any right, it only provides a good excuse. The plea of necessity does not imply a denial of law. According to Grotius, the doctrine of necessity is subject to certain general qualifications and limitations: there must be an absence of *mens rea* on the part of one who exercises the alleged right; there must be a real and vital danger; the danger must be imminent in point of time; the action must be no greater than is necessary for the particular object in view; and consideration must be given to the equities involved.[87] If the actions of the United States fell within these general qualifications and limitations, the requirement of request, under the extraordinary and emergency circumstances of the case, which would gener-

35

ally precede any right to land troops in the Dominican Republic may possibly be waived by the plea of necessity.

III. *THE ACTION OF THE ORGANIZATION OF AMERICAN STATES*

Measures in General

On April 28, 1965, when President Johnson announced the landing of United States forces in the Dominican Republic, he stated that the Council of the OAS had been advised of the situation by the Dominican Ambassador and promised that the Council would be kept fully informed.[88] On the following morning, at the request of the Representative of the United States, the Council met in a special session. After a review of the serious situation prevailing in the Dominican Republic and of the actions of the United States up to that time, it was resolved to request the Papal Nuncio in Santo Domingo, as Dean of the Diplomatic Corps in the Dominican Republic, to keep the Secretary General of the OAS informed as to what was transpiring in the Dominican Republic and as to the prospects for achieving an immediate cease-fire. During the night of April 29-30, the Council called upon all rival parties to agree to a cease-fire, to suspend all hostilities and military operations, and to establish an "international zone of refuge."[89] After being apprised by the Papal Nuncio of his efforts to achieve a cease-fire, the Council on the afternoon of April 30, dispatched the Secretary General to the Dominican Republic to work with the Papal Nuncio in peace-making efforts and to indicate to the Dominican people as well as to the world at large that the seriousness of the Dominican situation required the presence of the OAS.

At the request of the Chilean Representative, the Tenth

Meeting of Consultation of American Ministers of Foreign Affairs convened on May 1 under Articles 39 and 40 of the Charter of Bogota, i.e. to consider matters of an urgent nature and of common interest to the American states.[90] During its first plenary session, a five-man Special Committee was authorized to proceed to the Dominican Republic to do everything possible to reestablish peace. Specifically the Special Committee was to offer its good offices to obtain a cease-fire and an orderly evacuation of persons who had taken asylum in diplomatic missions as well as of foreign citizens. In addition it was to investigate all aspects of the situation in the Dominican Republic. Upon its arrival, the Committee found that the informal cease-fire which had been obtained earlier by the Papal Nuncio and the Secretary General was in serious jeopardy. The Committee sought and after much negotiation eventually obtained a new agreement from both sides, called the Act of Santo Domingo, which formalized the existing cease-fire, established a security zone to be respected by both groups, provided measures for the evacuation of asylees from foreign embassies, and made arrangements for the distribution of food and medical supplies.[91] On May 20, the Tenth Meeting, considering that the Special Committee had fulfilled its mandate, expressed its gratitude to the members for their service and entrusted the Secretary General with the continuing duty to seek to restore peace and normality in the Dominican Republic.[92]

On May 6, the Tenth Meeting adopted a highly controversial resolution[93] which requested governments of member states who were willing to do so to make available to the OAS contingents of their land, naval, air or police forces to form an Inter-American Peace Force which was to operate under the authority of the Tenth Meeting. Following this resolution certain United States contingents were withdrawn from the Dominican Republic and the remainder were incorporated into the Inter-American Peace Force under a unified command. Seven Latin American nations offered forces although, with the exception of Brazil, their numbers were small.[94]

On June 2, the Tenth Meeting took an additional step designed to lead to a political settlement in the Dominican Republic by appointing a three-man Ad Hoc Committee made up of representatives of Brazil, El Salvador and the United States. This Ad Hoc Committee had as its principle function that

of achieving the establishment of a climate of peace and reconciliation that will permit the functioning of democratic institutions in the Dominican Republc and its economic and social recovery.[95]

Through long months of agonizing work this Ad Hoc Committee eventually obtained signatures from both factions (the rebels now calling themselves the "Constitutional Government," and the loyalists calling themselves the "Government of National Reconstruction") on a document known as the Act of Reconciliation in which a provisional government was agreed upon, and on a document known as the Institutional Act which was to serve as the constitutional instrument under which the provisional government was to exercise its functions.[96] On September 3, 1965, Hector Garcia Godoy took office as Provisional President of the Dominican Republic and promised democratic elections within a period of six to nine months. Hope prevailed that civil strife would end, but the Provisional President has had a stormy incumbency for sporadic outbreaks of violence have marred the peace, requiring the continued presence of the Inter-American Peace Force.

Background to Legality

When the United States landed additional forces after evacuation of its nationals, one of its stated purposes in so doing was to preserve the capacity of the OAS to function in the manner intended by that organization's Charter to achieve peace and justice through securing a cease-fire and through reestablishing orderly political processes within which *Dominicans could choose their own government free from outside interference.*[97] The United States contemplated a multilateral collective action and participation by the OAS, viewing its own unilateral action only as a necessary prelude to give to the organs of that body the time necessary for a thorough consideration of the problem in order "to determine means of preserving the rights of that country under the inter-American system."[98] The United States, therefore, maintained that its armed landings were legal. Others have asserted them to be illegal, claiming that only through the multilateral action of the OAS in creating the Inter-American Peace Force, were the unilateral illegal actions converted into legalized multilateral action. Still others have asserted that an irregular use of force by one nation cannot be legally regularized by multilateral conversion and condonence.

Even if the original use of armed force by the United States was illegal, it has been said that the organ which is constitutionally competent to act can by later ratification regularize measures which might otherwise have been illegal. Such a view has been expressed in national constitutional law areas.[99] Whether or not this be true, or whether the OAS collective action was taken with no thought to ratification but was regarded solely as its own, to be justified the power exercised must be consistent with its instruments of creation and competency endowment—the Charter of the OAS and the Rio Treaty. With reference to the Dominican crisis, one uncontestable statement can be made: the OAS adopted a most unusual pattern of action, a pattern at variance with its proceedings in previous cases coming before it.

For an understanding of the role of the OAS in the Dominican case, it should be recognized that the Meeting of Consultation of Ministers of Foreign Affairs and the Council of the OAS each wears two hats. The Meeting of Consultation has, under Article 39 of the Charter of the OAS, two broad functions assigned to it: 1) to consider problems of an urgent nature and of common interest to the American states, and 2) to serve as the Organ of Consultation under the Rio Treaty in deciding upon the specific action to be taken in the field of security whenever a particular case arises. The Council of the OAS is the organization's permanent executive organ and is endowed with certain powers of a political, supervisory and coordinating nature as Council; but, in addition, it acts provisionally as Organ of Consultation under the Rio Treaty until the Organ of Consultation (the Meeting of Foreign Ministers) takes place.

Article 3 of the Rio Treaty requires that the Organ of Consultation shall meet without delay in the event of an armed attack by any state against an American state in order to agree upon the measures of collective character that should be taken by the American states. Article 6 of this treaty is even broader, requiring a meeting of the Organ whenever the inviolability or the integrity of the territory, or the sovereignty, or political independence of any American state is affected by an aggression which is not an armed attack, or by an extra-continental or intra-continental conflict, or by any other fact or situation which might endanger the peace of America. The Organ of Consultation is called upon in case of aggression to agree upon measures which must be taken to assist the victim of the aggression, or in any case on measures which should be taken for the common defense and for the maintenance of peace and security in the hemisphere. The decisions of the Organ or the Provisional Organ arising under Article 3 and

40

6 are legally binding upon the members. The obligatory effect of the decisions of the Consultative Organ is borne out by Article 20 of the treaty which declares that decisions requiring the application of measures specified in the treaty are binding upon all ratifying states, with the sole exception that no state is required to use armed force without its consent. Therefore when two-thirds of the voting members at a meeting acting as Organ of Consultation decide that the chiefs of displomatic missions shall be recalled from a country, that diplomatic or consular relations shall be broken, or economic relations, transport or communications be interrupted, each of the parties is bound to carry out the decision even though it may have voted against it. The Organ may also decide that it is necessary to use armed force. Although no state may be required to use armed force, this does not affect the validity of a decision by the Organ to use such force. It simply permits each state to decide of its own free will if it wishes to employ this measure in accordance with the decision. Use of armed force, after a decision by the Organ, would, of course, be legal if in harmony with the UN Charter.

To date there have been three convocations of Meetings of Ministers of Foreign Affairs acting as Organ of Consultation under the Rio Treaty, although there have been several disputes involving threats to the peace in which prompt action was needed.[100] In these latter cases the Council, invoking Article 6, called for a Meeting of Foreign Ministers but set no date for such meeting. Instead it declared itself to be provisionally the Organ of Consultation, and in all of these cases the prompt action of the Council as Provisional Organ made unnecessary the Meeting of Foreign Ministers as well as prevented these controversies from taking on a more dangerous character.

Had the Tenth Meeting of Ministers of Foreign Affairs been called as Organ of Consultation under the Rio Treaty, validity of its actions could have been easily justified. The ample provisions of this treaty and the precedents based thereon would cover the Dominican crisis and the OAS actions taken in relation thereto. In previous situations of aggression against an American state or of threats to hemispheric peace, the Organ of Consultation or the Provisional Organ has requested information from the contending parties, or has carried out its own investigations through the use of committees sent to the scene of conflict; has ordered disputants to abstain from further hostilities; has called upon each government to eliminate conditions which led to a dispute; and has made specific recommendations for settling the issue. Moreover it has requested the American governments to put at its disposal aircraft to make pacific observation flights over alleged battlefields; has ordered the interruption of diplomatic consular and economic relations with aggressor states; has expelled a member government whose actions were incompatible with the Organization's principles; and, in the Cuban missile crisis, even recommended the use of armed force.

As noted previously, the OAS has labelled assistance by a state to a revolutionary group in another state for purposes of subversion as being aggression and intervention. If this subversive intervention culminates in an armed attack by the rebel group, it can be said that an armed attack as visualized by Article 3 of the Rio Treaty has occurred. The Organ of Consultation is thereupon called to meet without delay to agree upon collective measures that should be taken to aid the victim. These collective measures can include the use of armed force which may be directed against the state to which the rebel group's attack is imputed, or, apparently, against the rebel group itself, or as otherwise necessary to avert or suppress the attack. A recommendation such as that which established the Inter-American Peace Force in a situation of collective self-defense can therefore be said to be valid under the Rio Treaty.

In past cases involving state participation in, sponsorship of, aiding or instigation of revolutionary or subversive movements directed against another nation, the Consultative Organs of the OAS generally acted under Article 6 of the Rio Treaty, called the activities aggression, and requested all other nations to take collective coercive measures of an economic or political charter against the government which was implicated. It is evident that the Organ of Consultation considers itself competent to take collective measures under Article 6 which are as broad as those it may take under Article 3. Some question might arise as to a call for the use of armed force under Article 6 if the illegal activity involved is, in the words of that Article, "an aggression which is not an armed attack." It has been asserted that the use of armed force is an execrise of self-defense, collective or individual, and is limited under Article 51 of the UN Charter and Article 3 of the Rio Treaty to repelling *armed attacks*.[101]

That the Tenth Meeting of Foreign Ministers could have taken all of their actions under the Rio Treaty is further strongly evidenced by a resolution adopted at the Tenth Inter-American Conference at Caracas in 1954; it was declared:

> That the domination or control of the political institutions of an American State by the international communist movement, extending to this Hemisphere the political system of an extracontinental power, would constitute a threat to the sovereignty and political independence of the American States, endangering the peace of America, and would call for a Meeting of Consultation to consider the adoption of appropriate action in accordance with existing treaties.[102]

This declaration was interpretative in nature, designed to assure that the broad terminology—"fact or situation that might endanger the peace of America"—of Article 6 of

43

the Rio Treaty which is repeated in Article 25 of the Charter of Bogota would include the domination or control by communists of an American government. The Organ of Consultation can in such a situation order necessary *measures* (which may include the use of armed force under the Rio Treaty). This resolution would have supported OAS action under the Rio Treaty in the Dominican case. Although the declaration does speak in terms of communist control or domination, its language could probably be interpreted to mean the prevention of such control or domination if there was an imminent danger thereof, for this too would be a fact or situation endangering the peace of the Hemisphere. Having recognized that control of an American state by communism is a threat to the sovereignty and political independence of that state and a danger to continental peace, the OAS should certainly be able to act to prevent the danger as well as to remove it after it occurs. Therefore if there was a potential danger of the establishment of a communist government in the Dominican Republic, the organization could resort to all the measures set out in the Rio Treaty.

Legality

Nevertheless the Council of the OAS did not convoke the Tenth Meeting of Ministers of Foreign Affairs to act as Organ of Consultation to study the situation in the Dominican Republic and thereafter to take the permitted measures under the Rio Treaty. In spite of the Caracas Declaration, some Latin American states denied that subversive interventionary tactics of an American communist state in aiding and fomenting revolutionary and guerrilla groups or terrorists acts in another state were acts of aggression so as to fall within the term of Article 6 and thus permit collective measures. The opinion was voiced that the OAS was not empowered to take measures, and cer-

44

tainly not forceful measures, to impede the establishment of a communist government in a member state. Such establishment through civil strife or *coup d'etat* or otherwise was a matter essentially within the domestic jurisdiction of a state, and the only competency of the inter-American system to defend the hemisphere against communism was to declare the philosophical basis of a communist regime incompatible with the principles of the OAS and to exclude such regime from participating in the organs of the OAS.[103] The resolution for the convocation of the Tenth Meeting of Ministers of Foreign Affairs carefully stipulated that the Meeting was called to consider the " [s]erious situation created by armed strife in the Dominican Republic."[104] This general and nebulous statement makes no mention of armed attack, aggression, extra-continental or intra-continental conflict, or threats to the peace of America, one of which would be requisite for an application of the Rio Treaty.

The hesitancy of some Latin American nations to proceed under the terms of the Rio Treaty can also be explained by the knowledge that non-forceful measures obtained by two-thirds vote would bind all member states. Other Latin American nations did not wish to proceed under the terms of the Rio Treaty because they were of the belief that if an aggression had been committed in the Dominican Republic it was an aggression by the unilateral action of the United States, and any proceeding under the Treaty should be directed against the United States. Whatever the reasons, political or judicial, the fact remains that the Council convoked the Meeting of Consultation under Article 39 of the Charter of Bogota which permits such convocation "to consider problems of an urgent nature and of common interest to the American States . . ." The urgent problem of common interest was set out to be the serious situation in the Dominican Republic created by armed strife. By proceeding in this manner, difficulties arise in attempting a legal justification of some of the actions of the OAS.

To begin with, a problem crops up as to the competency of the Council to take certain actions when it was sitting as Council. It was suggested, for example, during the night of April 29-30, that the Council adopt a resolution calling for an immediate cease-fire in the Dominican Republic and for the establishment of an international neutral zone of refuge. Had the Council been acting as Provisional Organ of Consultation under the Rio Treaty it would clearly possess all necessary political powers to act in accord with the express or implied powers granted. But it was objected that this resolution, to be taken when the Council was sitting as Council only, was beyond its power in that the resolution would be a first act of putting into effect an international peace-keeping procedure which was outside the Council's normal prerogative. Thereupon some changes were made in the wording of the resolution, *calling upon all groups* to pursue the possibility of a cease-fire and *urging* them to permit the establishment of a neutral zone. This changed resolution passed, but not unanimously.[105] On the afternoon of April 30, the Council adopted a resolution authorizing the Secretary General of the OAS to go to the Dominican Republic on a fact-finding mission and also to aid the Papal Nuncio in his attempts to make peace. The same objections were raised here.

In its resolution convoking the Tenth Meeting of Consultation, the Council called "attention to the provisions of Article 42 of the Charter of the Organization of American States." Article 42 reads: "If for an exceptional reason, a Minister of Foreign Affairs is unable to attend the meeting, he shall be represented by a special delegate." The Chilean Representative who requested the convocation declared that the urgency and gravity of the events which necessitated the meeting did not really permit the time necessary for the assembling of the Foreign Ministers of all nations, and, consequently, under Article 42 governments could appoint their representatives on the Council as the special delegates. Thus what came to pass was that the members of the Council continued to act in the Dominican case not as the Council but as the Tenth Meeting of Consultation of Ministers of Foreign Affairs. It can be argued that the framers of the Charter did not intend or did not contemplate such an interpretation of Article 42 which in effect did away with the necessity of any of the American Ministers of Foreign Affairs to participate in a so-called Meeting of Foreign Ministers. Article 42 was inserted mainly to permit the substitution of a special delegate on the rare occasion when a Minister for certain pressing reasons was not able to attend himself.

It was recognized by the framers of the Charter of Bogota that some matters could not await the cumbersome machinery of the Inter-American Conference to be brought into play, and, on that account, competency was granted to the Meeting of Consultation of Foreign Ministers to consider problems of an urgent nature and of common interest. A number of meetings have been called under this power, and, at these meetings, general resolutions and recommendations were taken, urging, requesting or suggesting that member states take certain actions. But, unlike such resolutions or recommendations under the Rio Treaty, even when adopted by a two-thirds vote they were not of a binding character. The power of a Foreign Ministers Meeting acting as Organ of Consultation under the Rio Treaty is a power of direct action—a power to prescribe a certain course of behavior by providing collective coercive measures to be taken in case of contrary behavior. These measures are excepted by the Charter of the OAS from the non-intervention principle and from the prohibitions against the use of force or of military occupation. A Meeting of Consultation acting under the urgent problem-common interest competency has broad powers to discuss, study, investigate and recommend, but these powers are not excepted from the basic OAS rules against the use of force or prohibiting intervention. If the OAS as a jural personality is obligated to respect these principles, it would be reasonable to assume that, in the absence of specific exemption, any attempt by a Meeting called under this competency to impose the collective will of the OAS and its members against a state without its consent would be interventionary in character and not legally permissible.[106]

During its first plenary session, the Meeting of Consultation sought to adopt a resolution creating a committee to proceed to the Dominican Republic to advise the contending military and police forces on matters relating to the establishment of a cease-fire, the suppression of hostilities, the evacuation of refugees and the restoration of peace and security. An immediate protest arose that this was an intervention and beyond the competency of the Meeting. Thereupon the wording was changed, limiting the committee to offering "its good offices" to all groups in the conflict. This passed as the mere offer of good offices was not considered an imposition of a collective will in that such offer could be accepted or rejected by the contending parties.

In June, when the Tenth Meeting appointed the Ad Hoc Committee, the same objection was raised to that portion of the resolution which permitted the Committee to provide the necessary directives to the Inter-American Peace Force. The Representative of Mexico, for example, took the stand that:

If the Committee which has been created were limited in its powers to offer good offices to the groups in conflict seeking to obtain a definite truce which can be converted into an established

48

peace, if it had been constituted outside the context of the resolution that created the Inter-American Peace Force, and if it were remote from the influence that the presence of foreign troops necessarily exercise upon the will and conduct of the Dominican people, my Delegation would give its approval; but this is not the case, and, in compliance with instructions received, I vote in the negative.[107]

Certain other Latin American countries, as well as Mexico, were highly critical of the legality of the resolution which established the Inter-American Peace Force. Its creation would have been legally unquestionable under the Rio Treaty in face of an armed aggression, but when organized by a Meeting called to consider problems of an urgent nature and common interest it left the OAS vulnerable to charges of usurpation of power. Although the Force was declared to have a sole purpose, in a spirit of democratic impartiality,

. . . of cooperating in the restoration of normal conditions in the Dominican Republic, in maintaining the security of its inhabitants and the inviolability of human rights, and in the establishment of an atmosphere of peace and conciliation that will permit the functioning of democratic institutions[108]

still some nations felt that its establishment was a prohibited intervention into a situation of domestic strife.

The resolution founding the Peace Force was carefully worded to avoid the implication of collective self-defense. It was stated that since the OAS was charged with the responsibility of interpreting the democratic will of its members, and that since it was obligated to safeguard the principles of its Charter, it was empowered to adopt appropriate measures in situations such as that presented by the Dominican Republic to assure reestablishment of peace and normal democratic conditions. As the OAS was competent to assist member states in the preservation of peace and the reestablishment of normal democratic conditions, it was also "competent to provide the means that reality and circumstances require and that prudence counsels as adequate for the accomplishment of such purposes."[109] It was therefore legitimate to form the Peace Force. This is indeed a very broad interpretation of some very florid language appearing in the fundamental instruments governing the OAS, wherein recognition is given to the ideals of political democracy and reaffirmation is made that the solidarity of the Americas requires the organization of the American states on a basis of representative democracy. It is doubtful that there is an international legal duty imposed upon the American nations to maintain a democratic form of government or that there is a right under the Charter of the Rio Treaty to intervene collectively to secure a democratic form of government in an American republic. The Charter of the OAS commands the American states to respect the rights of the individual, so it might be argued that an international duty within the Americas has come about to protect and guarantee human rights, but here again the OAS is not given a specific power to use coercive measures to establish human rights in a state which fails to live up to its obligations. Such action would then seem to be contrary to Article 15 of the Charter—the non-intervention edict.

However, an argument can be made to take the actions of the Tenth Consultative Meeting outside the concept of intervention. Some authorities distinguish collective intervention from collective action.[110] Any action taken by an international organization which is in the general interest of its members is not intervention. This may be acceptable providing the organization is acting within its legal competency. That the Tenth Meeting was so doing was strongly advanced by the Secretary General of the OAS who claimed that:

The purpose of the Inter-American Force is clearly not one of intervention but rather one of rendering assistance to the people of a sister nation.[111]

50

A similar stand was taken by the Malaysian Ambassador before the Security Council of the UN when he declared that the action in establishing the Peace Force was neither intervention nor enforcement action, but was a "conciliatory function," a type of action permitted to all international organizations to foster peace and tranquility and to permit a "people to establish a democratic civil government of their own choosing, to heal the wounds and the bitterness of civil strife, and to begin the path of relief and reconstruction."[112] If the Peace Force was not interventionary in character, the resolution creating it would be within the powers of the Tenth Meeting of Consultation.

A third position may be postulated, namely the theory that the mere existence of legal rules set forth in international agreements, no matter how excellent those rules may be, means nothing if they do not rest upon a community of ideology and interest. It was the sense of community which enabled the participating states to remove sources of possible conflict among themselves and to limit the application among themselves of their national sovereignty. The conditions essential to that sense of community are not the product of the rules set forth in treaties, but, on the contrary, ante-date such treaties. As the Costa Rican Representative pointed out, the strict interpretationists were in effect saying, save the rules even though the republic be destroyed.[113] But this ignored the basic reality that if saving the rules thereby destroyed the inter-American system as well as the Dominican Republic, the victory would be indeed hollow:

Within the anarchy and the disorder which reign in the Dominican Republic, no government can by itself maintain order and guarantee the difficult democratic process. Without the collective juridical action of the OAS there will be no more than two alternatives: either the permanency of United States troops, or the

51

triumph of the extremists and the establishment of a new communist dictatorship, incompatible with the Inter-American System, and fountain of subversive aggression against other governments of America, especially of the Caribbean region.[114]

This viewpoint then recognizes that despite the stress placed on the principle of non-intervention, the whole concept of the Organization of American States and all of the principles to which it is dedicated may, in certain circumstances, be more important and hence overrule the blanket proscription against intervention.

The Organization of American States Versus the United Nations

The Dominican crisis and the actions of the OAS with respect thereto were brought before the Security Council on May 3, 1965, and again gave rise to the twenty-year-old question of the respective roles of the regional and world communities in relation to peace-keeping, a question of proper jurisdiction, sharing of jurisdiction, and power to act. Two main issues are involved: should the situation or dispute be a subject of Security Council disposition if the regional organization is already seized of the matter? and what measures may the regional agency take to solve the problem in maintaining or restoring peace?

Inasmuch as the UN is the universal organization it has been asserted that even though a complaining state is a member of a regional organization which has already taken the matter under consideration, access to the Security Council is never barred. This is a right of all members to appeal directly to the world forum authorized by Article 33 of the UN Charter. Moreover, under Article 34 the Security Council may investigate a dispute or situation, and under Article 39 if it finds a threat to the peace, breach of the peace, or act of aggression it is authorized to decide upon proper measures to maintain or restore international peace. Even though Article 52 permits regional agency settlement and calls upon the Security Council to encourage settlement there through, this Article stipulates that it "in no way impairs the application of Articles 34 and 35." In the Security Council debates on the Dominican crisis it was stressed that the Security Council had primary responsibility for the maintenance of international peace which could not be supplanted by the actions of the OAS. The Uruguayan Representative to the UN affirmed that although certain precedents could be cited where the Security Council had decided to suspend consideration of a specific question pending a report from the OAS, at no time had the power of the Security Council to exercise the functions assigned to it by the UN Charter been challenged.[115] The activities of the regional system could not derrogate from the authority of the Security Council. This apparently was also the view of the present Secretary General of the UN, for in a press conference relating to the Dominican situation he declared that he viewed the peace-keeping operations undertaken by the OAS as possibly establishing an embarrassing precedent, implying thereby that the Security Council should have taken control of the case.[116]

A strong rebuttal to this thesis can be made for, although the Security Council is given the *primary* duty to maintain or restore peace, the International Court of Justice has pointed out that it is not the *only* body which may act when threats to the peace occur.[117] To the contrary, the Charter stipulates in Article 33 that parties shall first of all seek a solution by negotiation, enquiry, mediation, conciliation, arbitration, judicial settlement, *resort to regional agencies or arrangements,* or through other peaceful means of their choice. In addition the Security Council is enjoined to call upon the parties to resort to these means when it deems necessary. Article 52 exhorts parties to a regional arrangement to submit disputes for settlement to such

53

agency *before* referring them to the Security Council. *Before* is the operative word in this clause. Article 52 even requires the Security Council to encourage the pacific settlement of local disputes through regional agencies. The UN Charter recognizes the authority of the regional agency and, accordingly, regional agencies are an elemental part of the peace-keeping scheme of the Charter. Since the OAS and the UN have essentially the same goals it would seem that their missions are not mutually exclusive but are mutually reinforcing. This position has been affirmed by the majority of the American republics in earlier debates and was reasserted during the Security Council's discussion of the Dominican crisis by the Representatives of the United States. It was observed that in the past the

Security Council recognized the advisability of encouraging regional efforts, and its confidence in the abilities of regional organizations to deal with their own problems has been justified by the record.[118]

Attention was directed to the fact that the OAS had kept the Security Council fully informed of its activities as required by the UN Charter, and it was observed that as many of the nations of the UN had failed to pay their past-due legal expenses for peace-keeping operations, the budget of the UN might be in difficulty if that organization attempted to duplicate all of the work being carried on by the OAS in the Dominican Republic.

In order to end the debate on the primacy of rights between the regional and the universal organizations, the Representative of Jordan offered a resolution which was unanimously accepted:

The Security Council,
Deeply concerned at the grave events in the Dominican Republic,
1. Calls for strict cease-fire;
2. Invites the Secretary-General to send, as an urgent measure, a Representative to the Dominican Republic for the purpose of reporting to the Security Council on the present situation;

54

3. Calls upon all concerned in the Dominican Republic to co-operate with the Representative of the Secretary-General in carrying out his task.[119]

This compromise solution came under immediate attack. In a speech on the floor of the United States Senate, Senator Thomas Dodd of Connecticut commented:

The dispatch of two competitive peacekeeping teams to any crisis area violates the rules of common sense and diplomacy. If the United Nations team has simply come to the Dominican Republic for the purpose of supporting and paralleling the efforts of the OAS team, there would be no justification for its existence. And if the United Nations team has come to the Dominican Republic for the purpose of competing with OAS representatives, this creates a situation that can only do damage to the OAS, to the Dominican Republic and to the United Nations itself. Either way, the appointment of the United Nations team makes absolutely no sense.[120]

The Special Committee of the Tenth Meeting of Consultation, which had been entrusted with the duty of arranging a cease-fire and which had been given other responsibilities in the Dominican Republic, was also critical of the appearance on the scene of the UN Representative, because his intervention had a political effect which obstructed the progress of the Special Committee's negotiations with both factions.[121] The Director of the Department of Legal Affairs of the Pan American Union emphasized that although the jurisdiction of the UN and the OAS in the Dominican case was concurrent,

intervention by the world organization while the regional agency is making all possible efforts to reach a pacific settlement is a form of "abuse of power." The Security Council could very well, as it has done repeatedly in the past, have allowed time for the regional action to produce results, especially inasmuch as some results had already been attained. Furthermore, by the date of the Security Council's decision, the danger of the situation's affecting international peace and security had been averted. It is evident, then, that the Security Council made premature and undue use of its powers.[122]

The Netherlands Representative of the Security Council

55

adopted still a third position.[123] Article 52 (4) seeks to maintain the supremacy of the United Nations through the provision that resort to regional agencies or arrangements as permitted by Article 52 in no way impairs the application of Articles 34 and 35. Article 34 permits the Security Council to investigate any dispute or situation which might lead to international friction or give rise to a dispute, to determine whether its continuance is likely to endanger the maintenance of international peace and security. As to Article 35, any member of the UN is permitted to bring any dispute or situation to the attention of the Security Council. Thus if a member of the OAS refers a situation to the Security Council that body should limit its action to investigation in accordance with Article 34 and should continue to promote the regional settlement of the problem through the OAS. Only if the OAS fails in its attempts should the Security Council actively intervene.

The second aspect of the problem of the distinctive roles of the regional organization and the universal organization is concerned with the competence of the regional agency to decide upon collective measures, including the use of armed force to maintain regional peace. This arose in the Dominican affair with the establishment of the Inter-American Peace Force.

Article 51 of the UN Charter permits regional agencies to take measures in the exercise of the right of collective self-defense until such time as the Security Council takes the necessary steps to maintain peace. But in the Dominican crisis, the OAS did not base its action on self-defense. The term self-defense was carefully avoided. The resolutions adopted by the Council or the Tenth Consultative Meeting either referred to keeping the Security Council informed under Article 54 of the UN Charter which requires regional bodies to inform the Security Council of "regional activities," or, as in the case of the resolution creating the Peace Force, did not mention under which provision of the UN Charter the Security Council would be kept informed.

When a regional agency is not acting on a basis of self-defense, doubt is cast upon the validity of regional measures taken without Security Council approval for Article 53 of the UN Charter stipulates that no enforcement action shall be taken under regional arrangements without authorization by the Security Council. The validity of measures taken without prior authorization would then depend upon the definition given to the phrase "enforcement action."

It has always been maintained by the OAS that measures which do not involve physical violence can be employed at any time without prior authorization. Acting under Article 6 of the Rio Treaty in various cases of aggression or threats to hemispheric peace, the OAS has taken coercive diplomatic or economic measures of a non-violent nature against an aggressor state. Although these measures were reported to the Security Council, its prior authorization was neither sought nor felt to be required since they were non-forceful.[124]

Even though non-forceful measures may not fall within any definition of "enforcement action," there is strong support for the view that any use of physical force must fall within such definition, and, therefore, the use of physical force can only be legally taken with prior Security Council authorization unless it falls within the inherent right of individual or collective self-defense. Approached from this angle, the establishment and operations of the Inter-American Peace Force would be beyond the powers of the OAS as it was not acting in self-defense and as it had not obtained prior Security Council permission. Nonetheless, precedent exists for the use of force by the OAS without such authorization. In 1962, at the time of the Cuban missile crisis, the Provisional Organ of Consultation, acting under Article 6 of the Rio Treaty, recommended that the member states take individual and collective measures, including the use of armed force, to prevent Cuba from continuing to receive military material which threatened continental peace and security and to prevent the missiles already in Cuba with offensive capability from constituting an active threat to such peace and security. As a result, an armed quarantine of Cuba came into being. It was denied that this use of physical force was enforcement action; rather it was called an action destined to maintain peace in the hemisphere taken under the regional agency's co-jurisdiction with the Security Council over efforts to preserve peace.[125]

The International Court of Justice has vigorously limited the meaning of enforcement action. It declared that the activities of the United Nations Emergency Force, which had been sanctioned by the General Assembly, were not enforcement actions for they were undertaken with the consent of the states involved, and consent was the antithesis of enforcement which implied compulsion.[126] The Uruguayan Representative to the Security Council argued that the creation and actions of the Inter-American Peace Force must constitute enforcement action and could not be considered as a peace-keeping operation because in the case of the Dominican Republic, the Court's indispensable prerequisite of consent was missing.[127] However, he overlooked the fact that the International Court also held that the United Nations Operations in the Congo did not constitute enforcement action because such operations

did not include a use of armed force against a State which the Security Council, under Article 39, determined to have committed an act of aggression or to have breached the peace. The armed forces which were utilized in the Congo were not authorized to take military action against any State. The operation did not involve "preventive or enforcement measures" against any State under

Chapter VII and therefore did not constitute "action" as that term was used in Article II.[128]

This reasoning would support the legality of the Inter-American Peace Force for its purpose was not to take action against an aggressor state or against a government which by its policies was threatening peace. Indeed, the Tenth Consultative Meeting was acting under its Charter powers to consider matters of an urgent nature and of common interest, namely the serious situation created by civil strife in the Dominican Republic, and it could not have legally indulged in "measures which must be taken in case of aggression" for these are reserved for action under the Rio Treaty. In organizing the Peace Force there was no intent to take a preventive action or an enforcement action against any aggressor state or peace-breaking or peace-threatening nation. This was emphasized by the United States Representative before the Security Council when he pointed out that the OAS action in the Dominican Republic could not be equated with enforcement action but was, instead, action "against civil disorder, political chaos, bloodshed and internecine war."[129] This was echoed by the Malaysian Representative who called the work of the Peace Force a "conciliatory function."[130] Simply because an action may be accompanied by force does not make it an enforcement action, for it can happen that a pacific settlement operation may at times require a minimum use of force. He concluded that in the Dominican Republic the OAS was merely promoting peace and preparing the "necessary condition for the will of the people to find free expression so that it may ultimately prevail."[131]

IV. THE ACTION OF THE INTER-AMERICAN COMMISSION ON HUMAN RIGHTS

In the long slow development of international law, human rights have traditionally been the concern of the

59

individual state. Each state recognized rights for or withheld rights from its citizens according to its own concepts. Only since World War II has there been admission by the nations of the Western Hemisphere that this idea may be too restrictive, that human rights must be a subject of international concern for

governments which systematically disregard the rights of their own people are not likely to respect the rights of other nations and other people and are likely to seek their objectives by coercion and force in the international field.[132]

While the inter-American system has not as yet adopted legal norms from which human rights can be derived under positive law, it must be acknowledged that the Rio Treaty, the Charter of Bogota, and the American Declaration of the Rights and Duties of Man, which was adopted by the Ninth Inter-American Conference, have expanded the problem of human rights, at least partially, from the national to the international level by the assertions in all of these instruments that the observance of human rights is now a matter of international concern.

In 1959, the Fifth Meeting of Consultation of Ministers of Foreign Affairs created a seven-man Inter-American Commission on Human Rights charged with furthering respect for such rights.[133] The Commission was to have the specific functions that the Council assigned to it. In 1960, the Council adopted the Statute of the Commission, in which Article 9 sets forth its functions and powers as follows:

a) To develop an awareness of human rights among the peoples of America;

b) To make recommendations to the Governments of the member States in general, if it considers such action advisable, for the adoption of progressive measures in favor of human rights within the framework of their domestic legislation and, in accordance with their constitutional precepts, appropriate measures to further the faithful observance of those rights;

c) To prepare such studies or reports as it considers advisable in the performance of its duties;

d) To urge the Governments of the member States to supply it with information on the measures adopted by them in matters of human rights;

e) To serve the Organization of American States as an advisory body in respect of human rights.[134]

After the members of the Human Rights Commission were appointed, they debated the meaning of the Commission's competence. The majority decided that Article 9 (b) permitting them to make recommendations to the governments of member states *in general* should be interpreted to make *general recommendations* to individual member states.[135] Furthermore, even though the Statute did not mention power to receive and examine communications from individuals, the Commission resolved that under its power to prepare studies and reports it could take cognizance by way of information of written communications or claims received by it involving violations of human rights within the American states.[136] As there was some complaint in the Commission itself that these interpretations were illegal, the Commission proposed that its competence should be broadened so as to give it more power "since it felt that its obligation should not be limited simply to promoting respect for such rights, but rather it is obliged to see to it that they are not violated."[137] The Commission therefore drew up a series of requests to the Council suggesting that its Statute be amended so that its power to examine complaints of violations and prepare confidential reports, including recommendations to the government accused of violating human rights, would be unquestioned. The Council refused to amend the Statute, and thereupon the Commission interpreted its own competence to include not only the power to recommend the adoption of general measures in favor of human rights within the framework of the domestic legislation of each

61

state, but also to include the power to recommend to individual member states that they take the appropriate steps to further faithful observance of human rights. The Commission considered it proper to hear complaints by individuals and to request an accused government to give it information regarding the measures it was taking after the Commission had called its attention to specific violations.[138]

This interpretation was accepted by some states, disputed by others. Cuba, for example, declared that neither Article 9 (b) nor any other statutory provision authorized the Commission to concern itself with more than general legislative or regulatory measures, anything more was an illegal interference in the domestic affairs of a state.[139] The Commission replied that it had a right to interpret the legal precepts of its Statute in their "natural sense" which was derived from the basic principle that governed the function of the Commission, namely the mandate of the OAS to promote respect for human rights.[140] When the Commission sought, under its authority to hold its meetings in any American state when it so decides by an absolute majority of votes with consent of the government concerned, to hold a session in Haiti, that government refused consent on the grounds that such a session would be an interference in the internal affairs of Haiti.[141] Still, after the fall of Trujillo, the Dominican Republic permitted the Commission to investigate human rights in that nation and even requested it to return at a later date to see the improvements that had been made.[142]

Under its Statute the Commission was limited to discussion, study, investigation and recommendation, and, as can be gleaned, some nations hold that an exercise of any of these powers specifically directed at an individual nation amounts to intervention in internal affairs which is prohibited by both the UN and OAS Charters. These

62

states follow a line of authority which declares that the ban on intervention in internal affairs was meant to cover discussion, study and investigation; formal action by way of recommendation to a state within whose jurisdiction the subject matter lies; and certainly all enforcement action.[143] An acceptance of this idea would, of course, seriously curtail the Commission's power. Others dispute this interpretation saying that intervention is a technical legal word involving interference with the internal or external affairs of a state, without its consent, in an attempt to make the will of the interfering agent prevail. Whether discussion, investigation or recommendations are to be considered acts of intervention by the Commission would then depend on whether they were coercive attempts to maintain or alter existing conditions against the state's will.

Ordinarily discussion or investigation by organs of the OAS would not amount to intervention. Discussion and investigation are traditional methods of diplomacy and cannot be considered intervention so long as such discussion or investigation permits presentation of both sides of an issue and does not involve coercion. The fact that such discussion or investigation might mobilize against a nation whatever power may exist in the nebulous force of inter-American public opinion is insufficient to make it intervention, for to prohibit discussions or investigations would be to close virtually all channels of communication between the organization and states or among states themselves. But even if this is accepted, there is a possibility that discussion and investigation would fall within the aegis of intervention. Since a state might lose international prestige through the mobilization of public opinion against it, a discussion and investigation may have the effect of compelling that state to act in accord with the will of the Commission, even though no threat of other action is made. In such instances, if the Commission entered into a consideration, discussion or investigation directed against a specific state with the purpose of coercing that state to act in conformity with its will, this would seem to be interventionary.[144] The same may be said as to a recommendation. Ordinarily a recommendation of a general nature recommending a course or policy which all states of the OAS should follow would be within the authority of the Commission. But a specific censorious recommendation made against a state for the purpose of forcing that state's will would seem to be intervention.

Granting that discussion, investigation and recommendation might in some instances be interventionary in character, would such action always be violative of the nonintervention principle of the Americas? Some would say yes, others would disagree, pointing out that under the terms of the Rio Treaty the American regional community affirms as a manifest truth that peace is founded on the international recognition and protection of human rights and freedoms, and that the Charter of Bogota speaks of the duty of promoting respect for human rights and fundamental freedoms. This indicates that one of the major purposes behind the establishment of the inter-American juridical community was to bring about security and peace founded on law and on the protection of human rights. This fundamental purpose cannot be nullified by the nonintervention limitation of the Charter, for to do so would destroy the basic *raison d'être* of the inter-American system.

As has been stated, one important exception to the issue of intervention is the principle of consent. Prior or simultaneous consent is a valid basis for intervention.[145] As all the nations of the Hemisphere approved the Statute of the Commission on Human Rights, there can be no question but that they gave their consent to the portion of the Statute which empowers the Commission to prepare such studies or reports as it considers advisable. But did this imply that the nations gave their consent to permit the Commission to hear complaints by individuals charging violation of human rights by specific governments? Some hold that it does not, that when the Commission entertains such complaints, it is acting outside its authorized or constitutional power. Others would say that the preparation of studies and reports necessarily involves basic research, otherwise studies and reports are useless. In taking cognizance by way of information of individual claims against governments violating human rights, the Commission is merely engaging in basic research and the prior consent of the nations to the Statute would overcome any plea of illegality.

As to the Commission's power to make recommendations, feel that this can only be interpreted as prohibiting the Commission from singling out any particular member state in making its recommendation, and hence no consent was given to permit the Commission to make specific recommendations to individual members. The Commission itself interpreted its competence to mean that if it considered it advisable to make *general recommendations* to each individual member state, as well as to all of them, it might do so.[146] It assumed consent to this interpretation. There is yet another possibility here. It can be said that actually the Commission was defining the phrase *in general* under its dictionary meaning, that is *in general* means *for the most part*.[147] Under this reasoning, Commission recommendations would *for the most part,* generally or normally, be made to the governments of the member states, either individually or collectively, but if it so deemed necessary the Commission could make recommendations to other groups such as international bodies, non-governmental private organizations, or even such groups as organized rebels seeking to overthrow a government in power. This would mean that prior consent had been given for Com-

65

mission recommendations to individual governments.

Only under this latter interpretation, equating *in general* with *for the most part,* can the Commission's role in the Dominican situation be understood. For in that instance there were two groups, each claiming to be the legitimate government of the Dominican Republic, neither of which had been recognized by the OAS, yet the Commission made recommendations to both. If its power of recommendation were limited to recommendations to *governments only,* all of its work in the Dominican Republic would have been *ultra vires.* But under the dictionary interpretation the Commission may, when it deems necessary, give recommendations to other bodies.

The issue of consent is also of interest in that there was no consent from an accepted Dominican government for the Commission to enter Santo Domingo to carry on its investigations. Early in May, 1965, the "Constitutional Government" requested the OAS to send the Inter-American Commission on Human Rights to the Dominican Republic to investigate violations of human rights.[148] The same request was made by the "Government of National Reconstruction."[149] As neither of these was the established government, neither could speak for the nation, but since both requested the presence of the Commission, it can be implied that there was consent of the state. The Secretary General of the OAS also was of the opinion that the Commission should engage in such a study,[150] hence, the Commission went into the Dominican Republic with added competence under Article 9 (e) which permits it to serve the OAS as an advisory body on human rights. Before the Commission began investigating complaints, it recommended to each of the so-called governments that it agree 1) to respect and enforce the observance of the human rights set forth in the American Declaration of the Rights and Duties of Man; and 2) to extend to the Commission all facilities necessary for proper fulfillment of its mission. Each group signed a separate document accepting these obligations.[151]

After it addressed its request to the OAS, the "Constitutional Government" also sent a letter to the UN demanding the dispatch of the UN Commission on Human Rights to verify and take appropriate steps to stop violations of human rights allegedly being committed by the "Government of National Reconstruction."[152] It was this request that triggered the debate on the respective roles of the regional and world organization which ended not by sending in the UN Commission on Human Rights but rather by dispatching a representative of the UN Secretary General to the Dominican Republic. In Santo Domingo itself, at least as far as the relationship between the Representative of the UN Secretary General and the OAS Commission on Human Rights was concerned, the question of jurisdiction was functionally solved, for it was agreed that the Inter-American Commission would have charge of matters relating to investigation of violation of human rights and, in accordance with Article 54 of the UN Charter, which declares that the Security Council should at all times be kept informed of the activities undertaken by regional agencies for the maintenance of international peace and security, it was agreed that the OAS would continue to send in reports to the UN.[153]

Actually it is very difficult to understand exactly what the UN Commission on Human Rights could have accomplished in the Dominican Republic. In its first report to the UN, the UN Commission suggested that it be entrusted with the task of pointing out cases where a violation of human rights committed in one country could by its gravity, frequency, or systematic nature constitute a threat to the peace. This implied that the Commission would review petitions of individuals who felt that their human rights had been violated.[154] This report aroused such opposition in certain quarters of the UN on the grounds that such action would constitute an illegal intervention in the domestic affairs of a state,[155] that the following year the Commission laid down a general rule that it had no power to hear individual complaints concerning violations of human rights.[156] This has been the accepted policy of the UN Commission on Human Rights since 1947. It would have been a complete break with the long accepted interpretation of its competence if the UN Commission had sought to undertake any of the tasks which the OAS Commission carried on in the Dominican Republic.

According to Dr. Dunshee de Abranches, a member of the OAS Commission, in its initial stages this Commission accomplished the following:

a) Received and examined, up to August 30, 1965, 1105 denunciations, compaints and communications regarding violations;

b) Requested the competent authorities of the two governments to take pertinent measures to put an end to or prevent violations;

c) On various occasions visited all the prisons of the capital; and the majority of those in the interior of the country, as well as military and naval establishments, for the purpose of informing itself of the conditions under which the political prisoners were kept;

d) Managed to achieve, in some cases, that the conditions be improved; that the sick be attended; that the holding of some persons incommunicado be ended, and that prisoners who were held on mere suspicion be freed;

e) Requested the installation of Boards of Investigation and Review and the speeding up of their works, because of the precarious functioning of the organs of justice;

f) Addressed to the competent authorities, reports relating to executions and inhuman treatment of prisoners;

g) Attended to a large variety of special cases that were presented to it, as is shown in the partial reports prepared by the representatives of the Commission.[157]

Although certain members of the Security Council continued to press the UN Secretary General to instruct his Representative in the Dominican Republic to investigate alleged violations of human rights, the Secretary General pointed out that under the mandate given by the Security Council, his Representative was limited to observing and reporting. This did not cover investigation of complaints and charges about specific incidents of violation of human rights.[158] If the Security Council desired him to undertake such tasks, it would have to adopt a clarifying resolution. But even without a new resolution, one specific accusation was investigated by the UN Representative. Having received information from various sources concerning an alleged mass execution said to have been carried out by military and police elements of the "Government of National Reconstruction," at an estate known as "El Haras," the UN Representative visited the estate and found human remains as well as newly dug graves. He passed this information on to the Chairman of the Inter-American Commission and also to the UN Secretary General.[159] The Chairman of the OAS Commission immediately visited the scene, made arrangements for the Inter-American Peace Force to guard the area, and informed the OAS Secretary General.[160] The Secretary General, following an exchange of views with the Ad Hoc Committee, requested that a technical assistance mission composed of expert criminologists and organized by the General Secretariat of the OAS investigate and submit a detailed report.[161]

Upon its arrival in Santo Domingo on June 18, 1965, the three-man committee, working with the OAS Commission, obtained a staff to aid it, and began its investigations. Although the police and military officers of the "Government of National Reconstruction" offered aid to the Special Committee of Criminologists, none was forthcoming. Furthermore the Crimonogists found that "reticence and fear ... seals the lips of the civilian population."[162] The Human Rights Commission and the Special Committee of Criminologists finally established that approximately 42 persons had been executed. Members of the police or members of the army apprehended civilians, accused them of various offenses, and in supposed night time transfers to other prisons took them to various spots and shot them to death. The cadavers were often left unburied as a warning to others, although the local people generally buried them later.[163] The Criminologists placed the blame directly on the "Government of National Reconstruction" stating that in view of the evidence the authorities were well aware of what was happening.[164]

The Nuremberg Charter and judgment[165] are precedents for imputing criminal liability upon individuals for crimes against humanity such as were discovered in the Domincan Republic by the Criminologists. It has been argued that the Nuremberg Charter was merely an ephemeral measure enacted by the victor against the vanquished, but by a Resolution in December, 1946, the General Assembly of the UN unanimously affirmed the principles of international law recognized by the Charter and judgment of the Nuremberg Tribunal.[166] Dr. Schwarzenberger has pointed out that

The maximum of legal significance that can be attributed to this Resolution is that, in the future, any member of the United Nations will be estopped from contesting the validity of these principles as rules of international law.[167]

The OAS Criminologists accused the authorities of the "Government of National Reconstruction" of deliberately seeking to eliminate adversaries through a policy of mass executions without trial. Through their investigations the Criminologists were "in possession of the names of police and military persons accused of participating in the acts," although these were not released in the report for it was felt that they should be reserved "for the cognizance of the judicial authorities charged with applying punishment to those found guilty in the corresponding trial."[168] But the

70

potentialities of punishment within the Dominican Republic became moot on August 31, 1965, when both groups signed two documents, the Act of Dominican Reconciliation, which established a provisional government with the understanding that such government would proclaim a general amnesty under which no officer or enlisted man of the armed forces could be submitted to court martial or subjected to punishment of any kind for acts committed since April 23, 1965; and the Institutional Act, under which the general amnesty was extended to all persons who had committed acts under cover of the prevailing political situation.[169]

The Special Delegate of Colombia to the Tenth Meeting of Consultation, in a note addressed to the President of the Meeting, emphasized that the approval given to the articles contained in the Act of Dominican Reconciliation and the Institutional Act by the members of the Ad Hoc Committee of the OAS in Santo Domingo could not in any manner bind the American States represented at the Tenth Meeting.[170] The Ad Hoc Committee agreed, stating that, although it had assisted in the preparations of these documents, in its opinion neither the Meeting of Consultation nor the Ad Hoc Committee was a party thereto. In signing the documents, the Ad Hoc Committee certified that the parties agreed to comply with the terms. The documents were purely internal Dominican agreements and not intended to state legal principles of the inter-American juridical system.[171] Consequently it can be argued that if ever an appropriate forum can be established outside of the Dominican Republic, and if ever those guilty of crimes against humanity can be located outside the territory of the Dominican Republic, the internal general amnesty would not be binding, and the rules of international law established by the Nuremberg trials would come into play.

71

The Institutional Act required the provisional government to hold elections within a period of six to nine months and requested OAS cooperation in holding these elections including "the presence of the Inter-American Commission on Human Rights in the Dominican Republic, from the time of the entry into force of this Institutional Act until the elected government takes office."[172] The mission of the Commission, therefore, was not completed with the inauguration of the Provisional Government, as a matter of fact its mandate was extended. Where originally it sought only to secure the fundamental rights of life, liberty, personal security and physical integrity of individuals, now the Commission had the additional authority to concern itself with rights whose observance is essential for the effective exercise of the right to vote and the holding of free and democratic elections, such as those of suffrage, meeting, association and the like.[173]

At the Second Special Inter-American Conference, held in Rio on November 17-30, 1965, a resolution was adopted relating to the functions of the Inter-American Human Rights Commission. In view of the refusal of the Council of the OAS to clarify and extend the competence of the Commission by amending its Statute, even in face of a recommendation to do so by the Eighth Meeting of Consultation of Ministers of Foreign Affairs, the Rio meeting took the bit in the teeth and requested the Commission to conduct a continuing survey of the observation of fundamental human rights in each of the member states of the organization, and authorized it to examine communications submitted to it and any other available information

so that it may address to the Government of any American State a request for information deemed pertinent by the Commission, and so that it may make recommendations when it deems this appropriate, with the objective of bringing about more effective observance of fundamental human rights.[174]

72

It was ordered that the Statutes of the Commission were to be amended in accordance with the provisions of this resolution. In taking this action, the Conference was in effect giving binding force to the Commission's own interpretation of its competence. It is an established principle that any international body may initially interpret its own competence; however this autointerpretation is not a "decision" in that it is neither final nor binding. The final or binding decision belongs solely to the body which has the power to modify or suppress the original autointerpretation.[175] In case of the OAS this was either the Inter-American Conference or the Meeting of Consultation of Foreign Ministers. It might also be argued that since the Commission from its inception heard complaints from individuals and made recommendations to individual nations, it established a customary law precedent which was merely reaffirmed by the resolution of the Second Special Conference.[176]

The work and development of the Inter-American Commission contrasts starkly with that of the only other extant regional commission, the European Commission of Human Rights. The European Commission permits one government to accuse another government before the Commission of violation of human rights, and also permits any person, non-governmental organization, or group of individuals claiming to be the victim of a violation to appear before the Commission if the nation against which the complaint is made has declared that it recognizes individual petition and if the individual complainant has previously exhausted all local remedies.[177] This right of individual petition was the major contribution of the European Commission for it was the first acceptance by a group of states of the idea that an individual whose rights were denied should have a hearing by an international body. In spite of the fact that the European Commission has a firm treaty basis and was established much earlier than its Western Hemisphere counterpart, it can be questioned whether in actuality it has done as much to preserve human rights as has the Inter-American Commission. As far as handling individual complaints, it nowhere approaches the Inter-American Commission. For example, between July 1955 and December 1962, the European Commission received over 1700 complaints, but the majority were rejected by the Commission on the grounds that the applicant had failed to exhaust local remedies, or on the ground that the alleged violation took place before entry into force of the treaty, or because the alleged violation was not covered by the convention or for similar reasons. By the end of 1962 only twenty-seven individual applications had sufficient appearance of admissibility that they had been referred to the respondent governments for comment and "only seven individual applications had actually been declared admissible."[178] The far less rigid procedural restrictions on the Inter-American Commission have given that body far greater scope in handling individual complaints, and it has been seised of many more cases than the European Commission. One thing is certain, under its strict regulations the European Commission could never have handled a situation such as arose in the Dominican Republic. Thus all can be of one mind with the Brazilian member of the Inter-American Commission that:

The mission that the Commission was requested to accomplish in the Dominican Republic under special conditions constituted the most advanced and complete form of international protection of human rights ever described in the history of the law of nations and international relations.[179]

NOTES TO THE WORKING PAPER

1 As quoted by Kurzman, Santo Domingo: Revolt of the Damned 40 (1965).

2 Arceniegas, Caribbean Sea of the New World 38 (1946).

3 For discussions of the history of the Dominican Republic and the Island of Hispaniola see Arceniegas, *id.* at Chs. II, III, XVIII, XIX; Stuart, Latin America and the United States Chs. XI, XII (4th ed. 1943); Tansill, The United States and Santo Domingo 1798—1873 (1938); Welles, Naboth's Vineyard The Dominican Republic 1844—1924 (1928); Walker, Journey Toward the Sunlight Chs. I, II (1947). Articles on the 1916 United States intervention are found in Blakeslee (ed.), Mexico and the Caribbean 206 *et seq.* (1920).

4 For discussion of these cases and OAS action with respect thereto see I PAU, Inter-American Treaty of Reciprocal Assistance Applications 1948—1959, 70—154 (1964). See also Thomas & Thomas, The Organization of American States 299—302, 347—50 (1963).

5 On the impact of the Cuban revolution and this period in Caribbean history see Benton, "The Communist Threat at Our Back Door," N. Y. Times Mag., July 17, 1960, p. 10; Szulc, "Castro Tries to Export Fidelismo," N. Y. Times Mag., Nov. 27, 1960, p. 19; Thomas & Thomas, *id.* at 229—31, 316—21.

6 Request of the Government of Venezuela 1960, II PAU, Inter-American Treaty of Reciprocal Assistance Applications 1960—1964, 3—57 (1964).

7 For discussion of this period see Committee on Foreign Relations United States Senate, "Background Information Relating to the Dominican Republic," 89th Cong., 1st Sess. (1965); Kurzman, *op. cit. supra* note 1, at 39 *et seq.*; Szulc, Dominican Diary (1965).

8 See, e.g., Comments on the Dominican Republic by Senator Fullbright, Cong. Rec. 89th Cong., 1st Sess., vol. 111, No. 198—Part 2, Oct. 22, 1965. But see Address by the Honorable Thomas C. Mann, Under Secretary of State for Economic Affairs, Dept. State Press Release 241, Oct. 12, 1965.

9 *Ibid.*

10 The President of the Military Junta stated that "American lives are in danger and conditions of public disorder make it impossible to provide adequate protection, I therefore ask you [the United States Ambassador] for temporary intervention and assistance in restoring order in this country." As set forth in the First Report of the Special Committee, IV International Legal Materials 557 at 565 (May 1965). See also statement by President Johnson, April 28, LII Dept. State Bull. 738 (1965); Address by the Honorable Leonard C. Meeker, Dept. State Press Release 147, p. 3, June 9, 1965. The request for assistance has been a subject of controversy. Senator Fullbright alleges that the junta desired the intervention to prevent a communist takeover, but that the United States refused to honor a request unless it was couched in terms of the necessity of protection of United States citizens. Comments on the Dominican Republic by Senator Fullbright *supra* note 8, at 3. Moreover, it has been asserted that the United States solicited the request from the junta. Frankel, "Secret U.S. Report Details Policy Shift in Dominican Crisis," N. Y. Times, Dec. 14, 1965.

11 Statement by President Johnson, *ibid.*

12 Statement of Secretary of State, Dean Rusk of May 8, 1965 on communist subversion, The Dominican Crisis, Dept. State Pub. 7971, Inter-American Series 92 (1965). And see statement by President Johnson, April 30, 1965. LII Dept. State Bull. 742—43 (1965).

13 See, e.g., statements of the Soviet Union, Cuba and Uruguay before the Security Council, Report of tre Security Council, 16 July 1964—15 July 1965, GAOR:20th Sess., Supp. No. 2 (A/6002) at pp. 93—97 (1965).

[14] Thomas & Thomas, Non-Intervention: The Law and Its Import in the Americas 71 (1956).

[15] On legality of intervention in general see *id.* at 74—78.

[16] I Hyde, International Law Chiefly as Interpreted and Applied by the United States, sec. 73 (2d ed. 1947); Padelford, "International Law and the Spanish Civil Strife," 31 Am. J. Int. L. 226 at 228 (1937).

[17] See Hall, International Law 287 (6th ed. 1909); I Hyde, *ibid;* Garcia Mora, "International Law and the Law of Hostile Military Expeditions," 27 Fordham L. Rev. 309 (1958); Wright, "United States Intervention in the Lebanon," 53 Am. J. Int. L. 112 at 121—22 (1959). Another line of authority takes the position that a government commits no breach of international law by aiding the legitimate government at its request when insurgency occurs, and that, in general, impartiality or neutrality is not required until actual civil war (belligerency) comes into being. Fitzmaurice, "The General Principles of International Law Considered from the Standpoint of the Rule of Law," 92 Recueil des Cours 5 at 176—79 (1957); Padelford, International Law and Diplomacy in the Spanish Civil Strife 1—8 (1939); Pfankuchen, A Documentary Textbook of International Law 953—54 (1960).

[18] As to the equality of treatment doctrine of Latin America see Roth, The Minimum Standard of International Law Applied to Aliens 62 *et seq.* (1949); Shea, The Calvo Clause 18—19 (1955).

[19] The Uruguayan delegate before the Tenth Meeting of Consultation of Foreign Ministers denounced the United States action as violative of the above-mentioned provisions. PAU, Decima Reunion de Consulta de Ministros de Relaciones Exteriores (OEA/Ser.F/11.10, 8 Junio 1965) p. 4. The Colombian representative said that the only legal intervention was collective action. PAU, Consejo de la Organizacion de los Estados Americanos, Acta de la Sesion Extraordinaria celebrada el 29 de Abril de 1965 (OEA/Ser.G/11, C-a-569 (Aprobada) Parte II, 29 abril 1965) p. 13. See also the Soviet Union and Cuban denunciations in their statements before the Security Council cited *supra* note 13.

[20] On the minimum standard rule see Roth, *op. cit. supra* note 18, at 81 *et seq.;* Borchard, Diplomatic Protection of Citizens Abroad 177 (1915). Harvard Draft Convention on Responsibility of States by Reason of Damage Caused on Their Territory to the Persons and Property of Foreigners, 23 Am. J. Int. L. Supp. 133 (1929).

[21] Grotius, De Jure Belli Ac Pacis, Bk. III, Ch. II, V, at p. 627 of Classics of International Law (Scott ed. 1929).

[22] See the doctrines enunciated by Dr. Calvo and Dr. Drago both of Argentina and other efforts of Latin American statesmen and jurists to preclude such interventions as summarized in Thomas & Thomas, *op. cit, supra* note 14, at 339—44.

[23] PAU, Actas de las Sesiones Plenarias de la Sexta Conferencia Internacional Americana, 107—8 (1933).

[24] Statement of Ambassador Ellsworth Bunker before the Meeting of Consultation of Ministers of Foreign Affairs, April 30, 1965, PAU, Consejo de la Organizacion de los Estados Americanos, Acta de la Sesion Extraordinaria celebrado el 29 de Abril de 1965 Parte Segunda, (OEA/Ser.G/II, C-a-569 (Aprobada) Parte II, 29 abril 1965) p. 32.

[25] It is as Waldock says *prima facie* an intervention, although it may be justifiable as an exercise of the right of self-defense. Waldock, "The Regulation of the Use of Force by Individual States in International Law," 81 Recueil des Cours 455 at 467 (1952).

26 *Id.* at 493. Under the OAS Charter see Thomas & Thomas, *op cit, supra* note 4, at 162 *et seq.*

27 Art. 51, UN Charter. Arts 18, 19, OAS Charter. For discussion see Waldock, *id.* at 495 *et seq.*; Thomas & Thomas, *id.* at 162.

28 Waldock, *id.* at 503; Bowett, Self-Defense in International Law Ch. V (1958); Fitzmaurice, *supra* note 17, at 172—73. But see Brownlie, International Law and the Use of Force by States 298 (1963); Jessup, A Modern Law of Nations 169 (1948); de Visscher, Theory and Reality in International Law 159, n. 47 (1957).

29 This is the classic test which evolved from the case of the *Caroline.* II Moore, A Digest of International Law 412 (1906); see Jennings, "The Caroline and McLeod Cases," 32 Am. J. Int. L. 82 (1938). This definition was accepted by the International Military Tribunal at Nuremberg. The International Military Tribunal Nuremberg, cmd. 6964, p. 28 (1946).

30 Waldock, *supra* note 25, at 466—67; Bowett, *op. cit. supra* note 28, at 87 *et seq.* The Inter-American Treaty of Reciprocal Assistance (Rio Treaty) in its Art. 9 speaks of an unprovoked armed attack by a state not only against the territory, land, sea or air forces of another state but also against its people as an aggression.

31 Brownlie, *op. cit. supra* note 28, at 289; Bowett, *id.* at 91—94.

32 On Latin American attitudes see Shea, The Calvo Clause (1955).

33 Ross, A Text-Book of International Law 244 (1947). And see Bowett, *op cit. supra* note 28, at 88—90.

34 Ross, *id.* at 249.

35 However Kunz states in relation to Article 51 that it must be an armed attack made by a state, but he goes on to add "or with the approval of a state." Kunz, "Individual and Collective Self-Defense in Article 51 of the Charter of the United Nations," 41 Am. J. Int. L. 872 (1947).

36 See the definition of the *Caroline* cited in note 29, *supra.*

37 Address by the Honorable Thomas C. Mann, press release *supra* note 8, at 7.

38 Kelsen, The Law of the United Nations 791 *et seq.* (1950); see also Beckett, The North Atlantic Treaty 13 (1950); Kunz, *supra* note 35, at 878.

39 But see Kunz, *id.* at 876 for a different line of reasoning.

40 See Thomas & Thomas, *op. cit. supra* note 14, at 124.

41 Bowett, *op. cit. supra* note 28, at 184 *et seq.*; Stone takes a somewhat similar position. Stone, Aggression and World Order 94—97 (1958); see also Cheng, General Principles of International Law as Applied by International Courts and Tribunals 101 (1953).

42 See Higgins, The Development of International Law through the Political Organs of the United Nations 220—21 (1963).

43 See Fitzmaurice, *supra* note 17, at 173; Waldock, *supra* note 25, at 503.

44 As set forth by President Johnson in his statements of April 28, 30, 1965, LII Dept. State Bull. 738, 742 (1965).

45 See Fenwick, International Law 287—88 (4th ed. 1965); I Oppenheim, International Law 312—13 (8th ed. Lauterpacht 1955); Stowell, International Law 349 *et seq.* (1931). On the abuse of rights doctrine see Gutteridge, "Abuse of Rights," 5 Camb. L. J. 22, 25 (1935). Cases of humanitarian intervention are discussed briefly in Graber, Crisis Diplomacy 337 *et seq.* (1959).

46 Stowell, *id.* at 362.

47 See Parry, "Some Considerations upon the Protection of Individuals in International Law," 90 Recueil des Cours 652 at 702 (1956).

48 The statements of the United States Government concerning its coopera-

tion with Belgium in the Congo rescue operation are contained in LI Dept. State Bull. 838—46 (1964).

49 See Satow's Guide to Diplomatic Practice 177 (Bland ed. 1958). Collective intervention by several states took place in China during the Boxer Rebellion when the legations of several nations were attacked and the Ministers of Germany and Japan assassinated. See Brownlie, *op. cit. supra* note 28, at 33 for a short discussion.

50 As set forth in the statement of Ambassador Bunker, *supra* note 24, at 31.

51 "Report of the Sub-Committee (Of the League of Nations Committee of Experts for the Progressive Codification of International Law) on Responsibility of States for Damage Done in Their Territories to the Person or Property of Foreigners," 20 Am. J. Int. L. Spec. Supp. 177 at 182 (1926).

52 Many Latin American jurists stress the principle of non-intervention in a conflict with human rights or representative democracy. See, e.g., Quintanilla, Pan Americanism and Democracy (1952).

53 Thomas & Thomas, *op. cit. supra* note 14, at 91—97.

54 *Id.* at 374—90.

55 Art. 1 (3).

56 See statement of Secretary of State, Dean Rusk, as set forth in "Background Information Relating to the Dominican Republic," *op. cit. supra* note 7, at 26.

57 Address by the Honorable Thomas C. Mann, *supra* note 8, at 9.

58 See e.g. Comments on the Dominican Situation by Senator Fullbright, *supra* note 8, at 2 *et seq.*

59 See statement of the Soviet Union before the Security Council, Report of the Security Council, *op. cit. supra* note 13.

60 See statement of Uruguay, *ibid.*

61 I Hyde, *op. cit. supra* note 16, sec. 73.

62 Statement of Ambassador Bunker, *supra* note 24, at 33.

63 See Habana Convention on the Duties and Rights of States in the Event of Civil Strife, PAU, Treaties and Conventions Signed at the Sixth International Conference of American States, Habana, Cuba, Jan. 16—Feb. 20, 1928, pp. 19—20 (1950); Protocol to the Convention on Duties and Rights of States in the Event of Civil Strife, 1955—1957 Inter-American Juridical Yearbook 161—67 (1958). The latter has not been widely ratified. See also Thomas & Thomas, *op. cit. supra* note 4, at 345—52 for short discussion of OAS cases involving fomenting of civil strife as aggression. See also Request of the Government of Venezuela 1963—1964, II PAU, *op. cit. supra* note 6, at 181 *et seq.*

64 Resolution, "Communist Offensive in America," Eighth Meeting of Consultation of Ministers of Foreign Affairs 1962, II PAU, *id.* at 69.

65 *Ibid.*

66 *Ibid.*

67 *Ibid.*

68 Alfaro, "Memorandum on the Question of Defining Aggression," Yearbook of the International Law Commission, 1951, Vol. II, UN Doc. No. A/cN.4/L.8 at 37—38.

69 See Ninth Meeting of Consultation of Ministers of Foreign Affairs serving as Organ of Consultation in the Venezuelan-Cuban Affair which arose before the OAS in 1963. II PAU, *op. cit. supra* note 6, at 185—86.

70 *Ibid.* McDougal & Feliciano, Law and Minimum Public Order 190 (1961).

71 UN Doc. A/C.1/SR/61 (1947).

72 SCOR, 13th yr., 833rd mtg. (1958).

73 As contained in 5 Whiteman, Digest of International Law 319—20 (1965).

74 SCOR, 13th yr., 819th mtg. (1958).

75 5 Whiteman, *op. cit. supra* note 73, at 318.

76 Note 69, *supra*.

77 Christian Science Monitor, Nov. 1, 1965, p. 13.

78 Address by the Honorable Thomas C. Mann, *supra* note 8, at 9—10.

79 PAU, Special Consultative Committee on Security, "Report of the Special Consultative Committee on Security on the Work Done during Its Fifth Regular Meeting." OEA/Ser.L/X/II.10, Nov. 10, 1965, pp. 4—5.

80 Resolution, "Special Consultative Committee on Security against the Subversive Action of International Communism," II PAU, *op. cit. supra* note 6, 70 at 72.

81 *Id.* at 186.

82 Fawcett, "Intervention in International Law," 103 Recueil des Cours 347 at 369 (1961).

83 S/PV.1200 (5 May 1965) p. 11.

84 See note 10, *supra*. Friedmann, in "United States Policy and the Crisis of International Law," 59 Am. J. Int. L. 857 (1965) sets out the view at 868 that there was an absence of request from a government in the Dominican case and that the United States intervention therefore could not be justified. See also Beteta, "Independence Remains the Key Principle of Mexican Foreign Policy," The Latin American Times, Oct. 12, 1965, p. S—8.

85 Bowett advances such a position. See Bowett, *op. cit. supra* note 28, Ch. X.

86 Rodick, The Doctrine of Necessity in International Law (1928). Such a doctrine is often disputed and is generally limited to the necessity to act in self-defense only. See I Oppenheim, International Law 298 (8th ed. Lauterpacht 1955).

87 As set forth in Rodick, *id.* at 6 .

88 Statement by President Johnson, April 28, 1965, *supra* note 10.

89 1 The OAS Chronicle 1 (Aug. 1965).

90 PAU, Consejo de la Organizacion de los Estados Americanos, Acta de la Sesion Extraordinaria., *op. cit. supra* note 19.

91 Act of Santo Domingo is set forth in 1 The OAS Chronicle 28—29 (Aug. 1965).

92 *Id.* at 4, 25.

93 *Id.* at 23—24.

94 The actual number of troops and other contingents of the participating countries (Brazil, Costa Rica, El Salvador, United States, Honduras, Nicaragua, Paraguay) is set out *id.* at 5.

95 *Id.* at 5, 26—27.

96 PAU, Act of Dominican Reconciliation and Institutional Act, (OEA/Ser. F/11.10, Doc. 363, 7 Sept. 1965).

97 Address by the Honorable Leonard C. Meeker, *supra* note 10, at 3.

98 *Id.* at 4.

99 Lincoln apparently thought that certain measures taken by him in Civil War days could and would be later regularized by the Congress. Corwin, The President Office and Powers 157—58 (1941).

100 The Sixth Meeting in 1960 at the request of the Government of Venezuela, the Eighth in 1962 at the request of the Government of Colombia, and the Ninth in 1964 at the request of the Government of Venezuela. These Meetings as well as the applications of the Rio Treaty by the Council acting as Provisional Organ are contained in Inter-American Treaty of Reciprocal Assistance Applications, vols. I & II, *op. cit. supra* notes 4 and 6.

101 See authorities cited note 38, *supra*. For discussion of this issue see Thomas & Thomas, *op. cit. supra* note 4, at 264—68, 351—52.

102 Resolution XCIII, Tenth Inter-American Conference, Caracas, Venezuela

March 1—28, 1954, as contained in Report of the Delegation of the U. S. A., Dept. State Pub. 5692, pp. 156—57 (1955). Fenwick states emphatically that the Caracas Declaration covers the situation. Fenwick, "The Dominican Republic: Intervention or Collective Self-Defense," 60 Am. J. Int. L. 64 (1966).

103 Statement of the Special Delegate of Uruguay before the General Committee on May 3, 1965. PAU, Decima Reunion de Consulta de Ministros de Relaciones Exteriores, Acta de la Cuarta Sesion de la Comision General (OEA/Ser.F/11.10, Doc. 32, 27 mayo 1965) p. 20 at 21.

104 1 OAS Chronicle 19 (Aug. 1965).

105 Statements of the Representative of Uruguay before the Council. Acta de al Sesion Extraordinaria celebrada et 29 Abril de 1965, op. cit. supra note 19, at 41—43. There were four abstentions: Chile, Mexico, Uruguay and Venezuela.

106 On the competency of the Meeting of Foreign Ministers to consider problems of an urgent nature see Thomas & Thomas, op. cit. supra note 4, at 84—86. As to the powers to discuss, investigate and recommend as interventionary see id. at 166—68.

107 PAU, Decima Reunion de Consulta de Ministros de Relaciones Exteriores, Acta de la Decima Sesion de la Comision General (OEA/Ser.F/11.10, Doc. 131, 2 junio 1965) p. 17 at 19. With respect to discussion concerning the Special Committee see PAU, Decima Reunion de Consulta de Ministros de Relaciones Exteriores, Acta de la Segunda Sesion de la Comision General (OEA/Ser.F/11.10, Doc. 24, 27 mayo 1965). For protest of the Special Delegate of Ecuador see id. at 11—12. Chile abstained to the creation of the Special Committee. With respect to the creation of the Ad Hoc Committee there was one vote against and three abstentions.

108 Resolution "Inter-American Force," as contained in 1 OAS Chronicle 23—24 (Aug. 1965). For views of the various American republics see PAU, Decima Reunion de Consulta de Ministros de Relaciones Exteriores, Acta de la Tercera Sesion de la Comision General (OEA/Ser.F/11.10, Doc. 29, 27 mayo 1965); Acta de la Cuarta Sesion de la Comision General (OEA/Ser.F/11.10, Doc. 32, 27 mayo 1965). Chile, Ecuador, Mexico, Peru and Uruguay voted against the Force. Venezuela abstained.

109 Resolution "Inter-American Force," as contained in 1 OAS Chronicle 23—24 (Aug. 1965).

110 E. g. Lleras, "Report on the Ninth International Conference of American States," 1 Annals of OAS 25—27 (1949).

111 As quoted by Mr. Yost of the United States before the Security Council. SCOR, S/PV. 1220, 3 June 1965, p. 57.

112 SCOR, S/PV. 1222, 9 June 1965, pp. 67—68.

113 Statement of the Special Delegate of Costa Rica, Acta de la Cuarta Sesion de la Comision General, op, cit. supra note 108, at 10—13.

114 Id. at 13.

115 Statement of the Representative of Uruguay, Report of the Security Council, op. cit. supra note 13, at 96.

116 As set forth in Garcia Amador, "The Dominican Situation, The Jurisdiction of the Regional Organization," 17 Americas 1 at 3 (July 1965).

117 Certain expenses of the United Nations (Article 17, paragraph 2, of the Charter), Advisory Opinion of 20 July 1962: I.C.J. Reports 1962, p. 151 at 163.

118 Statement of the Representative of the United States, Report of the Security Council, op, cit. supra note 13, at 94.

119 SCOR, S/PV. 1208, 14 May 1965, p. 6.

120 As quoted by the Latin American Times, July 2, 1965, p. 2.

121 Report of the Security Council, op. cit. supra note 13, at 105.

122 Garcia Amador, *supra* note 116, at 3.

123 Report of the Security Council, *op. cit. supra* note 13, at 100.

124 See Inter-American Conference for the Maintenance of Continental Peace and Security, Rio de Janeiro, Report on Results of Conference, Submitted to the Governing Board of the Pan American Union by the Director General, pp. 41—42 (1947). An excellent discussion of the various OAS cases in relationship to the UN is that of MacDonald, "The Developing Relationship between Superior and Subordinate Political Bodies at the International Level. A Note on the Experience of the United Nations and the Organization of American States," 2 Canadian Y. B. Int. L. 21 (1964).

125 II PAU, Inter-American Treaty of Reciprocal Assistance Applications, *op. cit. supra* note 6, at 109 *et seq.* And see Chayes, "Law and the Quarantine of Cuba," 41 Foreign Affairs 550 at 556 (1963).

126 Certain expenses of the United Nations, *supra* note 117, at 170—71.

127 Report of the Security Council, *op. cit. supra* note 13, at 116.

128 Certain expenses of the United Nations, *supra* note 117, at 177.

129 Report of the Security Council, *op. cit. supra* note 13, at 117.

130 *Supra,* note 112.

131 *Ibid.*

132 Marshall, "No Compromise on Essential Freedoms," 19 Dept. State Bull. 432 (1948).

133 PAU, La Organización de los Estados Americanos 1954—1959, p. 12 (OEA/Ser.D/II.2 1959).

134 PAU, Inter-American Commission on Human Rights, Report on the Work Accomplished during Its First Session, Oct. 2—28, 1960, p. 9 (OEA/Ser.L/V/II.I, Doc. 32, 1961).

135 *Id.* at 10.

136 *Id.* at 13.

137 *Id.* at 11.

138 *Id.* at 12.

139 PAU, Inter-American Commission on Human Rights, Report on the Situation of Political Prisoners and Their Relatives in Cuba, p. 4 (OEA/Ser. L/V/II.7, Doc. 4 ,1963).

140 *Id.* at 6.

141 PAU, Inter-American Commission on Human Rights, Report on the Work Accomplished during Its Fifth Session, Sept. 24—Oct. 26, 1962, p. 9 (OEA/Ser. L/V/II.5, Doc. 40, 1963).

142 PAU, Inter-American Commission on Human Rights, Report on the Work Accomplished during Its First Special Session, Jan. 3—23, 1963, p. 11 (OEA/Ser. L/V/11.6, Doc. 18, 1963).

143 See, e.g., Preuss, "Article 2, Paragraph 7 of the Charter of the United Nations and Matters of Domestic Jurisdiction," 74 Recueil des Cours 553 (1949).

144 "The fact that states have banded together and formed an international organization places in that organization elements of power which single members of the international community can never possess to the same degree. Therefore any action within the scope of authority of an international organization will tend to be of a mandatory nature if the values at issue are important to the member state involved, for a threat of loss of these values may compel it to act in accord with the will of the organization." Thomas & Thomas, *op. cit. supra* note 14, at 71.

145 Ross, *op. cit. supra* note 33, at 243.

146 PAU, Inter-American Commission on Human Rights, *op. cit. supra* note 134, at 10.

147 "-*in general* . . . generally, for the most part . . ." Webster's New Interna-

tional Dictionary of the English Language 1044 (2d ed. unabridged, 1940).

[148] PAU, "The Dominican Situation," 1 The OAS Chronicle 1 at 6 (Aug. 1965).

[149] *Id.* at 7.

[150] *Ibid.*

[151] *Id.* at 8.

[152] SCOR, S/PV. 1208, 14 May 1965, pp. 2—3.

[153] UN Security Council, Letter dated 29 June 1965 from the Assistant Secretary General of the Organization of American States Addressed to the Secretary General of the United Nations transmitting preliminary report on the human rights situation in the Dominican Republic submitted by Dr. Manuel Bianchi, Chairman of the Inter-American Commission on Human Rights, to the members of the Commission. (S/6495, 2 July 1965).

[154] Journal of the Economic and Social Council, First Year, No. 29, p. 522 (13 July 1946).

[155] These arguments are condensed in Lauterpacht, International Law and Human Rights 239 (1950).

[156] UN Economic and Social Council Doc. E/259.

[157] Dunshee de Abranches, "A Special Protection of Human Rights in the Dominican Republic," p. 3 (Washington World Conference on World Peace Through Law, T 7/6, Sept. 15, 1965).

[158] SCOR, S/PV. 1223, 11 June 1965, p. 6.

[159] SCOR, Report by the Secretary General, S/6432, 11 June 1965.

[160] PAU, Inter-American Commission on Human Rights, Human Rights Situation in the Dominican Republic 11 (OEA/Ser.L/II.12, Doc. 2, 1965).

[161] SCOR, Cable Dated 16 June 1965 from the Assistant Secretary General of the Organization of American States Addressed to the Secretary-General of the United Nations, S/6448, 16 June 1965.

[162] PAU, Tenth Meeting of Consultation of Ministers of Foreign Affairs, (OEA/Ser.F/II.10, 11 July 1965), p. 5.

[163] *Id.* at 13.

[164] *Id.* at 18.

[165] See 22 Trial of the Major War Criminals Before the International Military Tribunal 465—66 (1948).

[166] UN, Resolutions Adopted by the General Assembly during the Second Part of its First Session from 23 October to 15 December 1946, p. 188, Resolution 95 (1), "Affirmation of the Principles of International Law Recognized by the Charter of the Nurnberg Tribunal," taken at the 55th Plenary Meeting, 11 December 1946 (1947).

[167] Schwarzenberger, "The Problem of an International Criminal Law," 3 Current Legal Problems 263 at 291 (1950).

[168] PAU, *op. cit. supra* note 162, at 18.

[169] For texts of these acts see PAU, Tenth Meeting of Consultation of Ministers of Foreign Affairs, (OEA/Ser.F/II.10, Doc. 363, 7 September 1965).

[170] PAU, Tenth Meeting of Consultation of Ministers of Foreign Affairs, (OEA/Ser. F/II.10, Doc. 313, 20 August 1965) p. 6.

[171] PAU, Tenth Meeting of Consultation of Ministers of Foreign Affairs, (OEA/Ser.F/II.10, Doc. 320, 23 August 1965) p. 2.

[172] Art. 51, Institutional Act, *op. cit. supra* note 96.

[173] PAU, Inter-American Commission on Human Rights, Report on the Work Accomplished During Its Eleventh Session (Special), July 21—23, 1965, p. 11 (OEA/Ser.L/V/II.12, Doc. 10, 1965).

[174] PAU, Final Act, Second Special Inter-American Conference, Rio de Janeiro, Brazil, November 17—30, 1965, Resolution XXII, "Expanded Functions

of the Inter-American Commission on Human Rights," p. 32 (OEA/Ser.C/I.13, 1965).

175 Gross, "States as Organs of International Law and the Problem of Auto-interpretation," in Law and Politics in the World Community, p. 59 (Ed. Lipsky, 1953).

176 "Unless we are prepared to abandon every principle of growth for International Law, we cannot deny that our own day has its right to institute customs . . . that will themselves become sources of newer strengthened International Law." Report to the President of the United States by Robert H. Jackson, Chief of Counsel for the United States, The Nurnberg Case 14 (1947).

177 The text of the Convention establishing this commission may be found in I European Yearbook 317—41 (1951).

178 These figures are cited by Robertson, Human Rights in Europe 58 (1963).

179 Dunshee de Abranches, *op. cit. supra* note 157, at 9.

PART TWO

THE FORUM

SUMMARY OF THE FORUM PROCEEDINGS

The speakers at the forum differed both on the facts and on the law. Their differences on the facts concerned primarily the nature and extent of communist influence on the 1965 Dominican revolt. On the law they disagreed over when self-defense is a permissible exception to normal rules against intervention inside another state, over whether the U.N. or O.A.S. had priority, and over the legality of one intervention to combat another intervention. There was, however, no dispute about the accomplishments of the Inter-American Commission on Human Rights in the Dominican Republic.

The precise issues arising in the debate are set forth below, with pertinent quotations from the speakers' remarks.

I. *QUESTIONS OF FACT*

1) *The nature and extent of communist influence.*

Mr. BERLE expressed admiration for the working paper by Professor and Mrs. Thomas, but considered certain factual additions ". . . necessary to understand what really was going on, if we are to discuss realities. We here deal seriously with international affairs, where life and death are at stake and not with interminable Byzantine legalistics without point or outcome.

"I ask you to take quasi-judicial notice of facts which are public knowledge. If I do not give all the documentation, it is for lack of time.

"The first fact is that, prior to October 1962, Russian armed forces were in Cuba, and had precipitated the missile crisis there. The end of that crisis left uninterrupted the intrusion of the Soviet Union, in conjunction with Cuba, into the Caribbean Sea. That fact produced a resolution of the American states on January 27, 1962, at Punta del

Este, 'to urge the member states to take those steps appropriate for their individual or collective self-defense
resulting from the continued intervention in this hemisphere of the Sino-Soviet powers, in accordance with the
obligations established in treaties and obligations such as
the charter of the Organization of American States and
the Inter-American Treaty of Rio de Janeiro.'

"The condition producing that resolution had not, has
not, changed. The resolution was adopted a little over two
years prior to the Dominican affair, and before the Cuban
missile crisis, which of course made the dangers plain.

"I also ask you to take notice of the fact that the announced policy of the Soviet Union and of Cuba was to
prosecute 'wars of liberation,' sometimes rightly called by
Professor Thomas and others 'indirect wars.' Further that
in 1963, such a guerrilla war was in fact being carried
foward in Venezuela, and that Venezuela had successfully
appealed for help to the Organization of American States,
though she did not request the use of inter-American force,
being able to handle it herself. Further that in January
of 1965, three or four months before the Dominican crisis,
a meeting on Latin American policy was held under the
auspices of the Soviet Union, resulting in a communique
published on January 5th, in *Pravda*. This announced
among other things that it was the 'sacred duty' of the
people of the Soviet Union to support wars of liberation in
Latin America, including among them the struggle in the
Dominican Republic.

"Following this policy, cadres of Dominicans went to
Cuba for training, first in the Sierra Maestre, and later in
Czechoslovakia as guerrilla cadre leaders. A contingent of
these had already returned to the Dominican Republic to
act in that capacity.

"The American ambaassador in Santo Domingo reported
that these groups were equipped with a plan, that their

88

intent was to take over the government of the Dominican Republic, that they were promised help by the Cuban government. That was his estimate on April 26th just prior to the American action we are considering tonight.

"Ambassador Bennett had to surmise. The detail of the plan, proving his surmise accurate, later appeared in the *World Marxist Review* for January of 1966. It confirmed his April estimate. The plan, it was stated by the Dominican Communist leaders who wrote the article, would have been successful had it not been for the landing of the American troops when they did."

A member of the audience questioned the reliablility of the *World Marxist Review* on this point: "Mr. Berle, of course, is a lawyer of great experience and has argued many cases in court, and I find it very difficult to understand why he should accept self-serving statements in Marxist journals as good evidence. He refers in particular to a statement by Dominican Marxists claiming that their strength among the people was great, and that they would have easily triumphed had it not been for American intervention. Clearly, this is not the case, and the statement is simply a self-serving one designed to create an exaggerated impression of communist strength in the Dominican Republic.

"Professor Berle then relied on the fact that certain Dominicans had been trained in Cuba overlooking the fact that vastly more Dominicans had been trained in the United States in Camp Leavenworth, among them Colonel Francisco Caamaño Deñó, the leader of the so-called rebel forces."

Mr. BERLE added to his detailing of additional facts that "any one of us could have listened in, as I did, to the Cuban Radio during those days, discovering that the Cuban Radio promised assistance in all possible ways, to one faction of the rebels in Santo Domingo City. This continued right through until the issue was decided. To complain that there was not an attack fomented from the outside would be to ignore the plainest facts. The President had to take that in consideration in making his decision."

Mr. FRIEDMANN scoffed at the emphasis on communism as a cause of revolt. "I must confess that as I listened to the eloquent pleas made both by Professor Thomas and Professor Berle, I did feel a little like Alice in Wonerland. It seemed to me that the picture painted bore little relation to the facts as I have understood them to be, and as I believe them to be borne out by the ample documentation.

"For one thing, neither gentleman mentioned the name of Juan Bosch. Neither of them said that what was happening in the Dominican Republic was a social revolution led by the man who had been the respected Social Democratic Prime Minister of that country, recognized by this country, who had obviously vast popular support, at least in the capital, and was leading a revolt against the successors of the military regime of Trujillo. Trujillo was surely one of the most bloodstained and despicable tyrants known to have ruled a small country, who murdered, persecuted and robbed thousands of his opponents, and died owning personally one-third of the wealth of that country, $800 million.

"There was not a word about the fact that in the Dominican Republic, as indeed in most of the Latin American countries, there is ample cause for social revolt and discontent, and that the military dictators are almost invariably allied with the defense of propertied interests in land and business concentrated in very few hands."

Mr. FRIEDMAN was not challenged by Mr. BERLE when he said that "this revolution, by the universal testimony of responsible correspondents and observers, was on the point of succeeding when the United States intervened." But Mr. FRIEDMANN quickly made clear how few communists he believed were involved. "All subsequent efforts and documentations have revealed no more than that, at most, some fifty-seven persons were alleged to ✓ have been communists. And that in a revolution which involved hundreds of thousands of people."

Mr. BERLE's view of outside communist interference was quite different: "It was not one revolt but two, as appears from the facts. I am a friend of Mr. Juan Bosch; I have known him for years. He had nothing whatever to do with the communist end of it. I am prepared to think some of his forces didn't.

"There was a quite separate current directed by the three communist parties. One of these was Castro communist, one stood in close relation to the Russians, and a third in close relation with the Chinese. These groups did have arms, they did have organization, and it was their operation which could very easily have succeeded. * * *

"Answering your question specifically, I am quite clear that so far as Bosch himself was concerned, and in the earlier stages so far as Caamaño Denó was concerned, the communists were not in it. I am personally convinced that within twenty-four hours the communist latent organizations had been activated. By the time the arsenals were opened, the communist groups were even better armed than they had been before. At the close of the Dominican rising this had become a three cornered war, and a very bloody one at that."

Mr. FRIEDMANN squarely denied Mr. BERLE's assertions on foreign communist action. According to Mr. FRIEDMANN," . . . no amount of research has revealed action organized by a foreign state as distinct from sympathy. Certainly the U.S. government has not made any such allegation." This denial was repeated in Mr. FRIEDMANN's closing when he said, "I don't think that any

91

official documents, whether the congressional collection, Senator Fulbright's report, or the statements of the government have ever produced or sought to produce any evidence that the Dominican revolution was organized by either the Soviet Union or Cuba, as distinct from the obvious fact that they would have welcomed a communist government there as they did in Cuba."

2) *The invitation for U.S. landings.*

There was no dispute among the forum panelists that the U.S. landings in the Dominican Republic in late April 1965 were invited. The situation when the invitation was issued, as well as the standing of its source, were much disputed.

Mr. THOMAS declared that the revolt ". . . was sparked in part by disagreement between two factions of the armed forces of that nation. By the fourth day of the revolution, the two sides, the two factions, were in an approximate stage of stalemate. The country was without an effective government, and anarchy and disorder reigned."

A member of the audience, describing himself as a former adviser of the Dominican "Constitutionalist Government" at the U.N., took issue with Mr. THOMAS' assertion of a stalemate, as well as over which side were the rebels. "During the first days of the revolution, there was no such stalemate. There was real and legal leadership exercised by the constitutional government headed by Dr. Molina Ureña. The authority of this government was challenged only by a group of rebels who operated in the San Isidro Base. The rebels, headed by Wessin, opposed the restoration of legal and constitutional government freely elected by the people. The rebellious military set up a military junta whose jurisdiction didn't extend beyond the walls of the San Isidro Air Force Base. And this was the junta which requested the assistance of foreign troops."

Mr. THOMAS, labeling the "constitutionalists" as the rebels, denied that there was ". . . recognizable leadership among the rebels at that time. A military junta formed by the anti-rebel group admitted its inability to cope with the actions of mobs and those in rebellion, and requested the assistance of the United States to protect its own and other foreign nationals. The United States thereupon landed 400 Marines on April 29, to escort its citizens and the citizens of other foreign nations from the Dominican Republic. On the following day President Johnson made the decision to reinforce the original contingent by sending in additional troops. Among the objectives of this additional build-up were the quelling of bloodshed and the restoration of order. But the primary motive was to prevent a Communist takeover and the establishment of a new communist dictatorship in the hemisphere."

The two stages in the U.S. landings described by Mr. Thomas were supported by separate requests, according to Mr. BERLE. "The first was a simple request for help in procuring order. The United States government felt it unnecessary to give direct reply. Later came a formal request from the military junta, stating in substance that they were faced with a movement against democratic institutions, that they considered it directed by communists, that there were excesses against the population, mass assassinations, sacking of property, and so forth, that instigations from Radio Havana and other Cuban sources were extreme, and that they therefore asked unlimited help from the United States."

The junta's standing to invite U.S. landings was defended by Mr. BERLE. "Actually the military junta in one form or another had been in control of Santo Domingo for two or three years. It was exercising all the governmental powers. An outstanding fact is that outside of Santo Domingo City it was in complete control. It therefore can hardly be said not to have been an 'established government', if you ever do have an 'established government' under attack. I personally do not think that the inherent right of self-defense is dependent on anyone's request; but if needed, there was such a request, by a government as well established as a government asking such assistance can ever be."

Mr. FRIEDMANN on the other hand was ". . . somewhat surprised to find Dr. Berle arguing, at least contingently, that here was a request by the incumbent government for assistance. It has now been fully documented that the U.S. Ambassador at the last moment, when it was clear that the U.S. would intervene with overwhelming force, urgently phoned one of his friends in the junta and said please send us a request for intervention.

"Whether the junta was the incumbent at that time is highly uncertain, and Professor Thomas himself has argued at various places in this paper that it was not. In fact, the absence of any government was I thought the only reason for the original intervention. Now, however, it appears that for the subsequent intervention we reincarnate an incumbent government."

Finally, Mr. FRIEDMANN asked whether Mr. BERLE was ". . . really prepared to stand by his doctrine that the request of an incumbent government is the reason and justification for intervention? Does he condemn the U.S. action in support of the rebels that upset the incumbent Guatemalan Government in 1954? Does he condemn that Bay of Pigs invasion which was designed to upset an incumbent government, though wisely, I think, withdrawn before irreparable damage was done and a war started that perhaps might continue to this day like the war in Vietnam. I believe this is a highly questionable doctrine, even if we should accept the dubious assertion that the junta, about to be destroyed when the U.S. intervened, was a functioning government at that time."

II. *QUESTIONS OF LAW*

Certain of Mr. THOMAS' statements of the international law of self-defense were generally agreed to, such as that "intervention to prevent injury to and to protect the lives of a state's nationals present in another nation was, under exceptional circumstances, recognized to be legitimate by customary international law." Mr. FRIEDMANN referred to the initial U.S. landings as ". . . designed to protect, in a state of chaos and revolution, the persons and properties of U.S. citizens, an intervention involving perhaps a battalion or two." He conceded that, while it is doubtful that even this is justified strictly by international law, there has been much support in the literature of international law for the proposition that in a temporary situation of chaos a nation is entitled to provide protection for its citizens." Mr. THOMAS added that ". . . if such protection falls within the concept of self-defense, it is excluded from the absolute non-intervention principle established by the particular international law of the Organization of American States treaties, as well as from the ban on the use or threat of force in the United Nations Charter."

Reply was also made by Mr. THOMAS, without dispute, to the contention ". . . that the United Nations Charter today limits the right of self-defense to actions taken after an armed attack has occurred. And since no citizen of the United States had actually been seriously injured in the Dominican Republic at the time of the first landings, the sending in of the marines was stated to be premature and precipitous. However, customary international law would permit the exercise of the right of self-defense in case of an *imminent* threat of armed attack. And as the United Na-

95

tions Charter acknowledges that the right of self-defense is inherent—that is, it is inalienable, that it is firmly infixed—it would seem that the Charter provisions on individual self-defense do not change the customary law, but rather are merely declaratory of that law, designed to preserve the right by neither limiting it, nor extending it."

Other points proved more disputable, especially the following:

1) *Can an Uprising by Local Communists be Considered Foreign Aggression so as to Permit Collective Self-Defense?*

Mr. THOMAS expounded a doctrine of "indirect aggression," whereby aggressor State A acts through citizens of State B against the government of B. "Violent acts of indirect aggression and subversion fomented from abroad have been characterized by the O.A.S. as armed aggressions which bring into play the inherent right of individual or collective self-defense. The force which comprises an armed attack may include not only a direct use of armed force, whereby a state operates through regular military units, but also an indirect use of force whereby a state operates through irregular groups or terrorists who are citizens but political dissidents of the victim state.

"As those accepting the communist ideology hold devotion to a foreign power, which overrides national loyalties, and as they view their fellow countrymen of opposing ideologies as the true enemy, the test of whether an armed aggression is fomented from abroad cannot be a test of nationality, but must be a question of where true allegiance lies. Consequently, communist domination of a situation of civil strife has been labeled not a mere internal domestic matter, but a foreign attack upon another state." Mr. THOMAS did not know ". . . whether you can say just when there is an imminent danger of a communist

96

takeover in a country like the Dominican Republic, a country with thirty-one years of dictatorship, fast falling governments since the dictator fell, and Castro right next door."

Mr. FRIEDMANN rejected ". . . the contention that a communist revolution, although Professor Berle admits that as such it is not illegal, is in itself evidence of an aggression: aggrsesion by whom? Not by a state, but by that ghost called world communism. And world communism miraculously takes many forms. It takes the shape of simultaneously, Cuba, China, the Soviet Union, perhaps Czechoslovakia, Hungary, East Germany, or any other of the communist states."

To Mr. THOMAS, however, factional splits in the communist world did not prevent indirect aggression, for ". . . although we may not have a monolithic communist system, we have possibly three, Cuba, China, and Russia, and I think all of them were directing themselves against the Dominican Republic at this time. How many communists are needed to bring about a serious threat of a takeover in this situation would be almost impossible to say. I think the danger was there." Mr. THOMAS stressed that as a result of indirect aggression and subversion ". . . one small nation has already gone. Another one may go. Where are we going to draw the line? Is Panama going? Is Venezuela going? Is Central America going? Are we waiting for communism to come to the Rio Grande? This is all I say. The risk is there, in my opinion."

Mr. FRIEDMANN on the other hand argued for ". . . a return to the plain unambiguous law which I think has been treated with a certain degree of contempt but is the wisest course. The law is that intervention in the affairs of another country, the occupation of its territory, the invasion of its sovereignty, is illegal , as indeed is patently clear from the language of both the United Nations Charter and the O.A.S. Charter, unless there is evidence of aggression by a third party. And such evidence is not simply the advent of a left wing government that may or may not have communist elements. We have to recognize, and this is an insight now spreading in government circles, recently clearly formulated by Ambassador Averell Harriman, who I think knows as much about world communism as anyone else, that the alleged monolithic character of a universal movement called world communism, even if it was once the truth, is now a myth, that there are today many types of communist states pursuing divergent national policies.

"If Russia and China were not in sharp conflict with each other, competing for influence everywhere, probably we would today be in World War III, and we might not be sitting here to debate this matter. There is clear evidence of robust independence in many communist countries, in Eastern Europe—and I have just been in one of them—whose independence is so strong that the Soviet Union has extremely limited control. The fact is that today communist and left-wing revolutions have a strongly nationalist character. It may be greatly in the interest of this country to recognize this fact.

"And lastly, do results justify a policy of stricter regard for international law? Where has the situation changed in favor of the United States in recent years? In Algeria, in Ghana and in Indonesia, where there was no foreign interference. And in the Dominican Republic today, nearly a year after the intervention, the United States is still in as uncertain a position with results as indefinite and with the situation as obscure as it was when these fateful decisions were made a year ago."

Mr. BERLE's position on the issue of foreign aggression was summarized in one sentence. "If we agree that an armed attack fomented from outside, though carried on by alleged revolutionaries inside, is an 'armed attack' within

98

the meaning of the Treaty of Rio de Janeiro, giving rise to the right of individual or collective self-defense by any American state, I maintain that such an attack on the Dominican Republic was going forward during the last week of April 1965." He then suggested a standard for judging decisions made by those on the firing line of foreign policy. "It was the honest judgment of the American government that this was the fact. They had adequate and reasonable ground for that attitude. Whatever we have learned since verifies the fact that such an attack was planned and under way." The standard was later restated: "International law grants the right of defense in case of attack. It requires, in determining whether or not you are attacked either directly or indirectly, that a government must exercise good faith. This I submit the government of the United States did."

Mr. BERLE touched on the legislative history of the applicable rule on defense against armed attack. "It is sometimes disputed that the indirect war technique, a plot from outside to be carried on inside, is an armed attack within the meaning of the Treaty of Rio. I can only say that when the Rio Treaty was drafted and proposed to the United States Senate, and likewise when the NATO Treaty, which contains substantially the same words, was proposed, that precise question was brought up. "It appeared first in the Dulles report recommending these treaties, and again in the colloquy between Senator Fulbright and Mr. Dean Acheson when the NATO Treaty, whose language is the same as the Rio Treaty, came up for ratification. Said Mr. Fulbright, 'Would an internal revolution perhaps aided and abetted by an outside state in which armed force was being used in an attempt to drive the recognized government from power be deemed an armed attack within the meaning of Article 5? This is in the nature of a coup.' Secretary Acheson: 'I think this would be an armed attack.' That statement is repeated several times in the testimony.

"The drafters of the Rio Treaty like the drafters of the NATO Treaty thus did foresee the possibilities of an internal operation which would have the effect of an armed attack. They had, in fact, only recently been dealing as you will find in your working paper with just such an attack carried out in Greece, at that time promoted by the Soviet Union."

Additional legislative history was adduced by Mr. BERLE. "The 'non-intervention clause' is invoked. I happen to know it fairly well. I drew the wording myself in Buenos Aires in 1936, and those words have been repeated right through the treaties today. They were, as Mr. Thomas' working paper accurately states, not designed to be the *only* law of the hemisphere. Defense, the right of a country to call for assistance, was a recognized exception. Or perhaps defense did not need to be an exception, since at that time the legal doctrine of intervention did not cover or deal with questions of defense or of alliance to resist attack.

"When we deal with the Dominican situation, we must recognize the fact of a cold war, an 'indirect war' loose in the hemisphere. Such wars had gone on elsewhere in the Caribbean, notably in Venezuela within a very short time. There was a propaganda declaration of such indirect war in the Dominican Republic, and in case of attack the United States was empowered by the Rio treaty to act in its own self-defense. I submit this is not a mere legalistic argument. Only a short time before, the United States had been faced with a missile crisis in Cuba. Defense here is not a Byzantine argument devised to justify an action. Indirect war was a reality in inter-American affairs as they stood in Venezuela in 1964, in Cuba in 1962, in the Dominican Republic in 1965."

100

Mr. BERLE conceded that ". . . there is no law of the Western hemisphere or anywhere else that prevents a state which chooses so to do from going communist. What is prohibited is enforcement on any state of such a regime by armed attack fomented from the outside." Later he added, "the fact that a country indigenously chooses to go communist I don't consider any violation of international law or any reason for us to invoke self-defense. I look forward to the time when the United States will find a state whose civilization is not based on private property and which is friendly to the United States instead of openly hostile."

One fact was called "crucial" by Mr. Berle in showing that the Dominican revolt was foreign aggression permitting collective defense. "This was the precise relation of the Cuban and the Russian combination in connection with the action going on in Santo Domingo. Now everybody runs away from that. And I don't think that is realistic, because this relation changes the whole situation. I don't think that the United States is attacked because a revolution may be communist. Foreign use of such a revolution changes the picture. The Cuban experience showed us that intervention of the Soviet Union there literally brought the world to the threshold of nuclear war.

"Anybody that knows anything about the Caribbean, knowing where Haiti is, knowing the threats that had been made both from Cuba and the Dominican Republic against Puerto Rico and the life of Muñoz Marin, knows there were far greater risks involved than the nature of the Dominican government. To play over and over again the 'poor little Santo Domingo' quatrain, is a plain perversion of the international situation at the time."

A question from the audience prompted Mr. BERLE to state, "if you wish an analogy, had the United States—the United Nations wasn't then in existence, of course—moved into Czechoslovakia to protect against the Hitler movement fomented from the outside, there would have been a real parallel. Hungary, I think, presents a different situation. So far as I know, the Hungarian revolution of 1956 was entirely indigenous. I know of no outside power which had stirred it up. It developed internally. There was as far as I can see no justification for any intervention from outside. You see the difference. The difference is precisely that the United States Government believed outside nations were fomenting a revolution which thus became an armed attack on the Dominican Republic. On this, I think, the question of law really turns."

Another audience member put the question whether ". . . we have any revolutions where there is not a foreign influence, because even in our own we see the foreign effect was decisive in the independence of the United States." Mr. THOMAS replied: "One that does come to my mind in recent times, and at least no foreign influence was asserted, was the revolution against Peron in Argentina. That seems to have been a purely Argentine revolution. But may I add with respect to the American revolution, and the French intervention, that the British declared war on the French."

2) *Did Aggression Against the Dominican Republic Allow U.S. Action to Protect the United States?*

Mr. FRIEDMANN ". . . was quite frankly surprised to see put forward seriously by both Professor Thomas and Professor Berle that this country was acting in self-defense. This is where I felt like Alice in Wonderland. Was this country, the mightiest country on earth, now committing several hundred thousand army, navy and air force men thousands of miles away while maintaining still the power to act elsewhere, was this country acting in self-defense

102

against a revolution led in one of the weakest and smallest neighboring states by a social democrat leader and former Prime Minister, even if some fifty known communists were associated? If that is self-defense, then I think we can throw the U.N. Charter, the O.A.S., and any vestige of international law out. 'When I use a word,' Humpty Dumpty said, 'it means just what I choose it to mean— neither more nor less.' "

From the audience came the question: "Must missile bases be constructed in a Caribbean country before a real threat to our country exists? Mr. FRIEDMANN replied: "This is the kind of question which it's almost impossible to answer because it's largely rhetorical. But if it is another formulation of the thesis that any communist movement, or any partly communist movement, is a threat to this country and therefore justifies intervention as a measure of defense, my answer is a resolute "no".

"For example, if toworrow there is a revolt against the government of General Castelo Branco in Brazil, or if Odinga prevails against Kenyatta in Kenya, or if there's another change in Indonesia, which would be admittedly much more dangerous, I repeat with all emphasis that if we are to maintain a modicum of international law, we have here a principle, and I thought to speak as one lawyer to other lawyers on the role of international law and of the United Nations. Any doctrine implied in this question that a threat to the world-wide interests of the United States from what is imagined to be a government hostile to the United States is I think totally incompatible with the United Nations charter."

Mr. FRIEDMANN climaxed his remarks with a reference to ". . . the to me, I confess, incredible suggestion that the revolution that took place was an act of attack against the United States, which justified self-defense. If that is to be the law of nations, then I do not see how I

103

can continue to teach international law at Columbia, or anywhere else."

A legal basis for the "incredible suggestion" was described by Mr. THOMAS. "Article 3 of the Rio Treaty, the Inter-American Treaty of Reciprocal Assistance, observes that an armed attack against an American state imposes upon the contracting American States an obligation to assist in meeting the attack upon request for aid by the victim. There was no such request by the Dominican nation for United States aid, since there was no longer a responsible government in the Dominican Republic which could speak for the whole nation. However, a careful reading of Article 3 of the Rio Treaty would indicate that each state is expected to defend itself **against an** armed attack. If anarchy prevents the state from countering an attack against its territorial integrity or political independence caused by indirect aggression and subversion, it would seem that any other American State could act in self-defense if some legal interest of its own were being invaded.

"Ordinarily, if one state is subjected to an illegal armed attack by a second, this would not be an invasion of the legal rights of the third. But the treaties of the inter-American system indicate that the close integration and solidarity among the American republics incorporate the concept that each state of this hemisphere has a legal right in the security of all the other states. Thus, when Article 3 of the Rio Treaty declares that an armed attack against an American state is an attack against all of the American states, it establishes that each nation suffers a violation of its own legal rights by such an attack and may exercise its right of collective self-defense to protect itself not only against its own injury but also against the injury of the victim nation.

"This being so, the communist domination of a situation of civil strife in the Dominican Republic was also an aggression against each nation of the hemisphere, including the United States. Since the United States suffered a violation of its legal rights, its own legal rights, it could exercise its right of collective self-defense to protect its own vital security as well as the vital security of the Dominican Republic without a request for aid from the latter.

"The allegation that the United States had abandoned the concept of collective action because it had intervened unilaterally without prior consultation with the O.A.S. was vigorously denied by Secretary of State Dean Rusk. He asserted that among the primary motives for the landing of forces was that of preserving 'the freedom of choice of the Dominican people until the O.A.S. could take charge and insure that its principles were carried out.'

"The United States contemplated that its own unilateral action would be supplanted by O.A.S. multilateral collective action. The unilateral measures were viewed as a way to give the organs of the O.A.S. the time necessary for a thorough consideration of the problem in order to determine the best means for preserving the sovereignty, political independence and right of self-determination of the Dominican people under the inter-American system."

Later Mr. THOMAS summarized the basis for U.S. defense of itself in response to aggression against the Dominican Republic. "If you have a situation of self-defense as I have described it, then I think there is a right for any nation of the Americas to act in its own and the other nations of the Americas' self-defense. The Rio Treaty states this: an attack against one American state is an attack against all of the American states, and each state shall come to the assistance of the victim state upon its request."

Mr. BERLE reiterated, in regard to danger to the U.S. itself, his theme of not substituting hindsight for the good-faith decisions of the moment. "Mr. Friedmann may think it was not dangerous for the United States. That is his opinion. I may think something else—that is my opinion. But that the judgment of the Government of the United States that there was danger was given in good faith and with adequate reason I think cannot be disputed. Remember, a contrary judgment prevailed in connection with Cuba after the Bay of Pigs. A year and a half later the United States and the world stood at the threshold of nuclear war. To say in the safety of this hall and this room that there was no danger is absurd. I have lived half my life in the Caribbean, and I know."

3) *Which had Priority, the U.N. or the O.A.S.?*

The U.N. Charter provides in Article 53 (1) that "... *no enforcement action* shall be taken under regional arrangements or *by regional agencies without the authorization of the Security Council* ..." At the same time under Article 33 (1) *"the parties to any dispute,* the continuance of which is likely to endanger the maintenance of international peace and security, *shall first of all seek a solution by* negotiation, enquiry, mediation, conciliation, arbitration, judicial settlement, *resort to regional agencies* or arrangements, or other peaceful means of their own choice." (emphasis added).

Mr. THOMAS felt that, "... as regional organizations are an elemental part of the peacekeeping scheme of the charter, with concurrent jurisdiction over regional problems, there would seem to be no reason why the O.A.S. should not, once it is seized of a matter and making visible progress, continue to act without the intervention of the Security Council. When the Security Council adopted a resolution sending into the Dominican Republic a representative of the Secretary-General of the United Nations, it was said to have been abusing its power."

Mr. FRIEDMANN on the other hand was ". . . amazed

at the proposition that the United Nations was disabled despite the clear language of Articles 34 and 35 from concerning itself in the Dominican situation. If regional organizations are supposed to supersede the United Nations charter, then we might as well openly say so and regard the United Nations as dead." Article 34, which is quoted in full in the Appendix, allows the Security Council to investigate ". . . any dispute, or any situation which might lead to international friction or give rise to a dispute . . ." Article 35 covers the raising in the UN of disputes, on the initiative of either member or non-member states.

Mr. BERLE asked, "in international crises do you want action, or do you want merely words? We can have all manner of delay and debate. We can have all kinds of reference from this body to that body, to the Security Council, to the Powers having veto and back again. Is that international law or international mockery? Unless there is capacity for preventive action, these rights that we speak of, those appeals to the United Nations, to regional peace-keeping bodies, to the Human Rights Commission of the Organization of American States, or to any other body are nothing but soul savers for people who like to dream but refuse to face reality."

4) *Did the O.A.S. Undertake "Enforcement Action"?*

As indicated, U.N. Charter Article 53 (1) forbids regional enforcement action without Security Council authorization. Mr. THOMAS traced the reasons why he felt enforcement was not involved despite intricate legal problems.

"Had the Tenth Meeting of American Ministers of Foreign Affairs been called as Organ of Consultation under the Rio Treaty, that treaty's ample provisions would have covered the establishment of the peace force as a collective measure of self-defense. But the resolution convoking the

Tenth Meeting made no mention of armed attack, no mention of aggression, or extra-continental conflict, or a threat to the peace of America, one of which would be requisite for an application of the Rio Treaty. Rather the meeting was called under Article 39 of the Charter of the O.A.S., to consider problems of an urgent nature and of common interest to the nations of the Americas, and such problem was stated to be 'the serious situation created by armed conflict in the Dominican Republic.'

"As the actions of the Tenth Meeting were not taken in self-defense, some doubt can be cast upon the validity of regional measures taken without Security Council approval, for Article 53 of the U.N. Charter stipulates that no enforcement action may be taken under regional arrangements without prior authorization by the Security Council.

"In acting under the urgent problem-common interest competency, the Meeting of Consultation has broad powers to discuss, study, investigate, and recommend, but it is not given power to take measures for collective self-defense; nor under this competency are its actions exempt from the O.A.S. rule against the use of force or the prohibition of intervention. The resolution founding the peace force was carefully worded to avoid the implication of collective self-defense or collective security. It was stated that since the O.A.S. was charged with the responsibility of interpreting the democratic will of its members, and since it was obligated to safeguard the principles of its charter, it was empowered to adopt appropriate measures in situations such as that presented by the Dominican Republic crisis, to assure the re-establishment of peace and normal democratic relations.

"Hereby the O.A.S. indicated that its actions in the Dominican Republic, including the creation of the peace force, were not to be considered in the nature of enforcement action, but rather would be viewed as measures destined to maintain the peace of the hemisphere taken under the regional agency's co-jurisdiction with the Security Council over efforts to maintain peace. It was pointed out that the Tenth Meeting was convened under the urgent problem-common interest competency, and, in organizing the Peace Force, there was no intent to take preventive action or enforcement action against an aggressor state or a peace-breaking or peace-threatening state.

"The Tenth Meeting could not have legally indulged in measures which must be taken in case of aggression, for these are reserved to it for action under the Rio Treaty only. The organizing of the Peace Force was a measure in the nature, so it was said, of a conciliatory function to promote peace in the Dominican Republic so that the will of the people could eventually prevail. A conciliatory measure cannot be equated with an enforcement measure, it has been said, even if it did necessarily require a certain amount of force. Consequently, prior authorization by the Security Council was not needed."

Such reasoning did not seem appropriate to Mr. BERLE. "I imagine you must have felt as I did, as you followed the nice legal distinctions here presented. There is a certain Byzantine quality in debating whether the Inter-American group was meeting as the Organ of Consultation under the Rio Treaty, or as the Organ of Consultation under the Organization of American States. They are the same people. They take instructions from the same governments. If the legality of an operation turns on such finespun distinctions, we are living in an unreal world."

Mr. BERLE drew a parallel familiar to U.S. lawyers. "In old common law pleading, the man with the soundest case in the world was thrown out of court because his lawyers had forgotten to put in the right words of art. I

109

suggest we cannot leave the rights of peoples, the safety of nations, to that kind of technicality."

5) *Does the Law Allow Intervention to Enforce Non-Intervention?*

Mr. THOMAS described the difference of opinion on whether the inter-American rule against intervention applies to the O.A.S. itself. "Assertion has been made that action taken by an international organization, which is in the interest of its members, is not intervention. This was the position of the Secretary General of the O.A.S., who viewed the formation of the Peace Force as a legal collective measure taken to preserve the rights of the Dominican people under the inter-American system. But such reasoning did not satisfy those members of the O.A.S. opposed to the Peace Force. Strictly construing the doctrine of non-intervention, it was declared that the original unilateral use of armed force by the United States was illegal, and that this irregular use of force could not be legally recognized by converting it into multilateral action."

Mr. THOMAS proceeded to analyze the concept of non-intervention in terms of its underlying purpose. "Over a century ago, John Stewart Mill pointed out that the adoption of an absolute doctrine of non-intervention was exceedingly dangerous, unless accepted by all governments. He declared: 'The despots must consent to be bound by it as well as the free states. Unless they do, the profession of it by free countries comes to this miserable issue, that the wrong side may help the wrong, but the right must not help the right. Intervention to enforce non-intervention is always right, always moral, if not always prudent.'

"In the Dominican crisis of 1965, the measures taken by the Government of the United States indicated an awareness of the fact that the effects of non-action can well be more interventionary than the landing of troops to prevent the establishment of a communist dictatorship. Not to use power in the interests of peace and freedom may be a misuse of that power, just as much as bringing influence to bear on the wrong side of the issue.

"Despite the stress placed on the principle of non-intervention, the acceptance of collective responsibility by a majority of the members of the O.A.S. is an indication of a growing realization that the non-intervention principle is not the only inter-American principle. It must be relegated to its proper place. It is meaningless without a consideration of its harmony with the total legal and political system of the Americas. To raise it as the only rule of law in the Americas is to permit absolute non-intervention to defeat the very ideals non-intervention sought to protect, namely the liberty and self-determination of people.

"The strict constructionists who insist that the nations of the Western Hemisphere may not protect their survival with preventive intervention or even with counter-intervention when the vital goals of the inter-American system are at stake, are, in the words of the Costa Rican delegate to the Tenth Meeting, demanding that the rules be saved even though the republic be destroyed. Had their counsel been heeded in the Dominican crisis, the end would have been sacrified to the means."

Later Mr. THOMAS added the view that ". . . when the Monroe Doctrine was formulated, it was not to be considered as available to a monarchy or junta. It was really meant to protect democracy, both internal and external self-determination. And this would include democracy. This is the way I would see it. I must be realistic and tell you that it does not in all cases today protect democracy."

Mr. FRIEDMANN's reply began by dismissing Mr. Thomas' authority John Stuart Mill as ". . . a very great man, but not I think a leading authority on the inter-

111

national law of 1966. And Dr. Berle ranged from the lawyer to the statesman to the political philosopher arguing in terms, I think, of power and dynamics of action as much as of law. Ladies and gentlemen, we do stand here as lawyers in honor of a man deeply committed to the strengthening of law in international affairs. A little less than a year ago, the distinguished legal advisor to the State Department, Mr. Meeker, in defending the legality of the U.S. action, said very much like Professor Thomas and Professor Berle, that black and white cannot portray the situation in world politics.

"We all know that many legal situations are open and subject to different interpretations but law *is* ultimately a matter of black and white, or we should have no business to sit here and profess to be lawyers, whether in government, as practitioners, or as professors. I submit we must find an answer in terms of right and wrong.

"In national affairs that is undoubted, but in international affairs, as has been demonstrated tonight by two very distinguished lawyers, law is not taken quite so seriously, because consciously or unconsciously, there is always in the background the thought: 'right or wrong, my country.' International law is fine as long as it can be used as a point of argument, but it can be dismissed or twisted if the argument doesn't support the position of one's country.

"I think that far more people than would admit to it do regard international law in that way. And I respect the frankness of a man like Mr. Acheson, who has repeatedly declared that in matters of national crisis international law plays no part. I would rather go along with that view, though I believe it to be quite inadequate to the tasks of our generation, than with the manipulation of legal argument.

"And certainly here in the Hammarskjöld Forum,

where we are to commemorate the memory of a man dedicated to the service of international law and international order, we should take international law seriously, though not in a starry eyed manner. Hammarskjöld knew that the role of the United Nations, and any attempt at international order, is still largely an aspiration, that it has to struggle constantly against the realities of power.

"But there *are* norms of international law. If we wish to ignore them, then let us say frankly that international law is of no concern to us. But don't let us pretend that we argue in terms of international law, when in fact we argue in terms of power or of ideology.

"For that reason, I view with some apprehension the observation made by Dr. Berle that we should think in terms of action, not words. I think that as a legal argument this is perilous, because whether we like it or not, law is based on words, words formulated in statutes, in treaties, in conventions, in customary law."

III *THE INTER-AMERICAN COMMISSION ON HUMAN RIGHTS IN THE DOMINICAN REPUBLIC*

Dr. Durward V. Sandifer, U.S. member of the Inter-American Commission on Human Rights, was prevented from appearing at the Ninth Hammarskjöld Forum by an unforeseen meeting of the Commission in Mexico City. He sent a statement for presentation at the Forum. On hearing the statement summarized, Mr. BERLE commented that the Inter-American Commission's action ". . . came not only into Santo Domingo, but into the practice of civilization. A pale copy of this Human Rights Commission exists in the Council of Europe, but I know of no other part of the world where a similar body has claimed effective jurisdiction."

Another observation made at the Forum on the Inter-American Commission's standing was that "we are all too familiar with oppression of private citizens by police. And we are familiar with the consequent desire on the part of private citizens to have some third party to whom to turn, be it a review board, or an ombudsman, or what have you. But something happened in February of this year in the Dominican Republic, turning the tables around the other way, which may be unprecedented in the history of human affairs, and which adds tremendously to the stature of the Inter-American Commission on Human Rights. Believe it or not, the chief of the national police of the Dominican Republic in February 1966, after a series of brutal attacks upon members of his force by armed civilians, actually sent an appeal to the Inter-American Commission on Human Rights to protect his armed policemen against the attacks by civilians."

Dr. Sandifer's full statement follows.

The Inter-American Commission on Human Rights
in the Dominican Republic
June 1965 to June 1966
prepared by
Durward V. Sandifer, Member of the Commission
for the
Hammarskjöld Forum on the Dominican Crisis
New York City, May 2, 1966

Initiation of Activities

On May 10, 1965, the Inter-American Commission on Human Rights received a cable from the National Congress of the Constitutional Government requesting the visit of a representative of the Commission for the purpose of verifying on the spot "the abuses to which defenseless citizens were being subjected". On May 24, Dr. Jottin Cury, Minister of Foreign Affairs of the Constitutionalist Government, addressed the Chairman of the Commission requesting the transfer of that body to the Dominican Republic for the purpose of verifying, and of adopting the pertinent measures with regard to the "abuses and assassinations committed by the troops of the Government of National Reconstruction".

The Government of National Reconstruction likewise urged the Commission to make an on-the-spot examination of the situation regarding human rights in the Dominican Republic.

Concurrently, the Secretary General of the Organization of American States in a cable of May 25, 1965 from Santo Domingo to the President of the Tenth Meeting of Consultation of Ministers of Foreign Affairs of the American States, Ambassador Guillermo Sevilla Sacasa, declared:

"In view of numerous denunciations of violations of human rights formulated by both parties, I consider essential and urgent the presence in Santo Domingo of the Inter-American Commission on Human Rights. To facilitate here the work of that Commission I am informing and requesting cooperation of both parties."

Responding to these requests and without delaying to convene the members of the Commission, Professor Manuel Bianchi of Chile, Chairman of the Commission, proceeded from Santiago to Santo Domingo on June 1, 1965. There he joined the Executive Secretary of the Commission, Dr. Luis Reque, who had arrived from Washington the preceding day .

The Commission has since maintained a continuous presence in Santo Domingo through its Chairman, various members of the Commission and officers of its Secretariat. It has maintained its headquarters in the Hotel Embajador, adjacent to those of the Organization of American States and of the Ad Hoc Committee of the Tenth Meeting of Consultation.*

The foundation within the Dominican Republic for the work of the Commission was promptly established through two documents signed by the Chairman with the authorities of the two competing governmental authorities. That with the Constitutionalist Government dated June 8, provided:

"It is the duty of the Constitutionalist Government to affirm to the Inter-American Commission on Human Rights that:

"1. It has respected and will continue to respect the human rights established in the American Declaration of the Rights and Duties of Man proclaimed at the Ninth International Conference of American States, held at Bogota, Colombia, in 1948.

* OAS, *Report on the Activities of the Inter-American Commission on Human Rights in the Dominican Republic.* (June 1 to Aug. 31, 1965) **OEA/Ser.L./V/**II.13, Doc. 14. Oct. 15, 1965.

"2. It has respected and will continue to respect, basically, the right to life, the right to trial by competent courts, the right to protection from arbitrary arrest, and the right of every person to humane treatment during the time he is in custody.

"3. It will provide to the Inter-American Commission on Human Rights, or to the representative of the said Commission, all of the facilities that are essential for the proper fulfillment of its mission".

In the other, dated June 9, the Government of National Reconstruction reaffirmed to the Commission that

"Faithful to its purpose to comply with the requirements of the Constitution of the Republic, especially those with regard to human rights, and all the international commitments assumed by the Dominican Republic, it has respected, it will respect, and it will enforce the human rights established in the American Declaration of the Rights and Duties of Man approved by the Ninth International Conference of American States, held at Bogota, Colombia, in 1948.

"Consequently, the Government of National Reconstruction will continue, as it has done up to now, to furnish the Inter-American Commission on Human Rights all of the facilities that are essential for the proper fulfillment of its mission."

Former Activities of the Commission in the Dominican Republic

It was not accidental that the Commission was thus invited to launch in the Dominican Republic its first major operational undertaking in support of human rights. It had previously undertaken two visits to the Dominican Republic with the consent of the Government, and the mem-

117

bers of the Commission, as individuals, had participated in the Symposium on Representative Democracy, sponsored by the Government in Santo Domingo in December, 1962, on the eve of the elections. The members of the Commission with the other participants in the Symposium, had at the invitation of the Government acted as observers of the election on December 20, 1962.

The two visits mentioned were taken under authority of Articel 11c of the Commission's Statute which authorizes it to "move to the territory of any American state when it so decides by an absolute majority of votes and with the consent of the Government concerned". The first visit took place October 23-27, 1961, with the approval and cooperation of the Government of President Joaquin Balaguer, "for the purpose of examining the situation in the country" with reference to the observance of human rights. In a note to the Government dated November 8, 1961, later published in its Report, the Commission commented in detail on violations of the rights of life, liberty and personal security, protection from arbitrary detention and arrest, freedom of investigation, opinion and expression, participation in political parties and elections, inviolablity of the home, and freedom of education. The Report concluded:

"From the facts and observations contained in this Report and in the Commission's note of November 8, it can be deduced that the most flagrant violations of human rights in the Dominican Republic were perpetrated during the time of the regime headed by Generalissimo Rafael Leonidas Trujillo. While the situation with respect to human rights improved after July 1, 1961, and new legislation was passed containing reforms designed to bring this about during the government of President Balaguer, serious violations

118

continued, as pointed out in this Report and in the aforementioned note of the Commission."*

The second visit from May 4-9, 1963, was at the invitation of the Government of President Juan Bosch, and related principally to alleged serious violations of freedom of speech and from arbitrary arrest and detention. After giving careful consideration to all information developed, the Commission concluded in its note of May 20 to the Secretary of State for Foreign Affairs:

> "The Commission refrains from qualifying the acts reported in the aforementioned cable, particularly the political aspects that such acts could imply, because of the conviction that the clarification of these acts properly belong to the administration of justice of the Dominican Republic, and furthermore, because the Attorney General of the Republic has informed the Commission that the investigation of these acts was in the stage of preliminary court proceedings.

> "The Commission understands quite clearly the full significance of the trust shown by the Dominican government in inviting it to meet again in Santo Domingo. The Commission hopes that the Dominican people will continue to enjoy the benefits of representative democracy recently established, and of the human rights upon which the existence of democratic government depends."**

Thus when the troubles of April-May, 1965 broke, both the public officials and the people of the Dominican Republic had unusual familarity with the nature and work of the Inter-American Human Rights Commission. That

---

* OAS, *Report on the Situation Regarding Human Rights in the Dominican Republic*, OEA/Ser.L/V/II.4, Doc. 32, May 22, 1962.

** *Report of Work Accomplished during Sixth Session*, OEA/Ser.L/V/II.7, Doc. 28, Aug. 21, 1963.

they turned to the Commission in their hour of crisis is perhaps a tribute to its impartial performance in its previous activities in the country. In the months that have followed in the midst of the opprobrium heaped indiscriminately on the representatives of the OAS, the Inter-American Peace Force, and the United States, it has not been unusual to hear the Commission's representatives popularly called "los buenos"—"the good ones".

Functions and Powers of the Commission

The Inter-American Commission on Human Rights was established by the Council of the Organization of American States in May 1960, pursuant to a resolution of the Fifth Meeting of Consultation of the Ministers of Foreign Affairs of the American States at Santiago in August, 1959. The Resolution called for a Commission "charged with furthering respect for such (human) rights", and the Statute approved by the Council declared it to be "an autonomous entity of the Organization of American States, the function of which is to promote respect for human rights". The rights for which it is responsible are "those set forth in the American Declaration of the Rights and Duties of Man" adopted at Bogota in 1948.*

The source of the Commission's authority to carry on activities of the scope and character it has been engaged in in the Dominican Republic is not immediately apparent on the face of Article 9 of the Statute defining its competence:

"In carrying out its assignment of promoting respect for human rights, the Commission shall have the following functions and powers:

"a. To develop an awareness of human rights among the peoples of America;

---

* *Final Act*, Aug. 12-18, 1959, OEA/Ser.C/II.5 (1960).

"b. To make recommendations to the Governments action advisable, for the adoption of progressive meas- of the member states in general, if it considers such ures in favor of human rights within the framework of their domestic legislation and, in accordance with their constitutional precepts, appropriate measures to further the faithful observance of those rights;

"c. To prepare such studies or reports as it con- siders advisable in the performance of its duties;

"d. To urge the Governments of the member states to supply it with information on the measures adopted by them in matters of human rights;

"e. To serve the Organization of American States as an advisory body in respect of human rights."*

The authority must be sought in paragraph 9b, as in- terpreted and applied by the Commission, combined with the use of Article 11b, noted above. At its first session in October, 1960, two different interpretations of paragraph 9b were put forward by members of the Commission. On the one hand, it was maintained that the correct interpreta- tion is that the Commission is limited to making recom- mendations to the governments of member states in general and that it may not do so to member states in particular. On the other hand the view was strongly supported that the Commission is empowered to direct its recommenda- tions to one or several states as well as to all of them to- gether, according to whether the violations are of a general or particular nature. The Commission ruled that the pro- vision empowers it "to make general recommendations to each individual member state, as well as to all of them".**

---

* *Basic Documents,* OEA/Ser.L/V/I.4, Rev. Aug. 26, 1963.

** *Report on Work of First Session,* Oct. 3-28, 1960, OEA/Ser.L/V/II.1, Doc. 32.

This interpretation was later combined with the Commission's assertion of the right to review conditions in individual countries where flagrant and persistent violations of human rights obtain, and to make findings or recommendations concerning them. The practice flowing from these broad assertions of competence has exercised a profound influence upon the nature of the Commission's work, as well as upon its stature in the Inter-American Community. A substantial part of its attention and time has been devoted to the review of conditions in individual countries.

In addition to its two visits to the Dominican Republic the Commission has requested and been denied permission to hold parts of sessions in Cuba, Haiti and Nicaragua. The Chairman and the Executive Secretary made an exploratory visit to Paraguay August 11-15, 1965 with a view to a possible visit of the Commission to that country. Ecuador and Honduras have expressed an interest in having the Commission come to their territory but the pressure of other activities has not made it possible to develop an opportune time. In the cases of Cuba and Haiti the Commission prepared and published reports on the basis of available information. Denied access to Cuba the Commission held part of a special session in Miami, with the approval of the Government of the United States, to gather information from refugees concerning the treatment of political prisoners in Cuba. The resulting Report on the "Situation of Political Prisoners and Families in Cuba" stands as a telling indictment of the behavior of the Cuban Government.[*]

---

[*] Cuba OEA/Ser.L/V/II.4 Doc. 30 (1962) and OEA/Ser.L/V/II.7 Doc. 4 (1963); Haiti—OEA/Ser.L/V/II.8 Doc. 5 (1963); Paraguay—OEA/Ser.L/V/II. 13, Doc. 5, Sept. 30, 1965. In the case of Nicaragua, the Government at first agreed in principle to a visit and then withheld consent when the Commission insisted on a time prior to the Nicaraguan election. *Report on Work of First Spec. Session.,* Jan. 1963, OEA/Ser.L/V/II.6 Doc. 18 (1963).

Thus when the invitation came from the two Governments in the Dominican Republic in May, 1965, the Commission had established itself as an action body with powers of specific recommendation, not limited to studies and reports. Its asserted competence to make reports and recommendations concerning conditions in individual countries seemed firmly established despite the instances of negative reaction by three countries. This conclusion is confirmed by the affirmation and expansion of the Commission's powers at the Second Extraordinary Conference at Rio de Janeiro in November, 1965, to be noted later.

Basis for Presence and Action of the Commission

It appears from the foregoing analysis that the Commission had laid a foundation for visitation, examination and recommendation with respect to conditions involving flagrant and persistent violations of human rights in individual countries. Nevertheless, from the beginning of the Dominican case, the President, the individual members of the Commission, and the Commission itself were confronted with an emergency situation reaching beyond the confines of the Commission's normal procedural and substantive law. The urgent demands of the situation in terms of human suffering, the national and international pressures for action, and its own history and approach of a maximum exploitation of its powers all pointed in the direction of making the "law fit the crime".

While the Chairman is authorized by Article 3b of the Regulations "to represent the Commission", this could hardly have been envisaged to cover the variety of situations confronting him in the early days of June in Santo Domingo. Yet he did not hesitate to negotiate with the two Governments, sign Agreements with them, use his good offices to help people to places of safety, investigate multifarious charges of violations of human rights, deal

123

with the Procurador General (Attorney General), military commanders, prison commandants, etc.

A subcommittee of the Commission, set up originally to review communications at the beginning of regular sessions, was convened by the Chairman in Washington June 20-23, 1965, to review his activities in the Dominican Republic as representative of the Commission. By taking note of the President's Preliminary Report, *On the Situation Regarding Human Rights in the Dominican Republic,* the Sub-Committee in effect approved his actions, and by suggesting that he "continue to act in accordance with his powers until a special meeting of the Commission is held to deal exclusively with the Dominican case", it endorsed his doing so.*

The Commission, convened by the Chairman in special session in Washington, July 21-23, 1965, adopted two resolutions, one covering action until a Provisional Government should be established, and the other the activities thereafter until the holding of an election. The first resolution authorized the Chairman "in accordance with his powers and by whatever means he considers most appropriate, to maintain a representation of the Commission in the Dominican Republic so that it may continue its attention to the problems related to human rights in that country in the course of the present situation". In justification for this action it declared the Commission had "a mandate to promote respect for human rights in all member states of the Organization"; invoked article 11c of the Statute authorizing it to meet in the territory of member states with their consent; cited Article 3 of the Regulations listing as one of the duties of the Chairman "to represent the Commission", and Article 8 providing that Members of the Commission during recesses "shall carry out the task

* OEA/Ser.L/V/II.12, Doc. 2, June 23, 1965.

or preparatory work entrusted to them"; and called attention to the agreements of June 8 and 9 of the two Governments to give all facilities to the Commission "essential for the proper fulfillment of its mission".

The second resolution was comparable in approach, authorizing the Chairman to maintain representation of the Commission after the establishment of the Provisional Government and until the holding of elections, provided the Institutional Act authorized its presence and the Provisional President requested it. In support of this the resolution cited the Draft Institutional Act contemplating the presence of the Commission until the installation of the elected government, and the need expressed at various times by the two Governments for the presence of the Commission "until the present situation in the country becomes normal".*

When the Commission met in Washington for its Twelfth Regular Session, October 4-15, 1965, it had to consider the question of its continued presence in the Dominican Republic in view of the installation of the Provisional President, García Godoy, on September 3, 1965 pursuant to the *Act of Dominican Reconciliation,* and the *Institutional Act* of August 31, 1965. The Institutional Act provided in Article 51:

"1. The elections shall be free in order to reflect the will of the Dominican People. The provisional government will request the cooperation of the Organization of American States in election preparations and the electoral process. This cooperation will include the presence of the Inter-American Commission of Human Rights in the Dominican Republic, from the time of the entry into force of this Institutional Act until the elected government takes office.

---

* *Report of Work of Eleventh* (Special) *Session,* July 21-23, 1965, OAE/Ser.-L/V/II.12. Sept. 20, 1965.

125

"2. The provisional government will undertake to cooperate with the Commission to enable it to observe compliance with the provisions contained in Part Two of this Institutional Act."

By Article 13 of the Institutional Act the Provisional Government pledged itself "to respect and enforce respect for the human rights and fundamental freedoms set forth in the American Declaration of the Rights and Duties of Man of the Organization of American States and the Universal Declaration of Human Rights of the United Nations". The substance of the rights contained in the American Declaration was embodied in Part II (Articles 15 to 48) of the Institutional Act in order to ensure strict compliance with the above undertakings (Article 14).*

In a note of September 27, 1965, the Vice Minister of Foreign Affairs of the Provisional Government, acting under instructions from his Government and pursuant to Article 51 of the Institutional Act, requested the Commission "to remain in the Dominican Republic until the installation of the Government selected in the forthcoming elections". He declared that the Commission "could count upon the full cooperation of his Government for the purpose of assuring the faithful observance of the provisions concerning human rights and fundamental freedoms contained in Part II of the Institutional Act.

After a thorough examination of the responsibilities which acceptance of this invitation would entail, the Commission stated the basis for its continued presence in the Dominican Republic in the following Resolution, which it is important to consider in its entirety: The Commission resolved—

---

* *Act of Dominican Reconciliation and Institutional Act,* OEA, Tenth Meeting of Consultation, Doc. 363, Sept. 7, 1965.

"IN VIEW OF:

"The invitation that has been extended to it by the Provisional Government of the Dominican Republic, in accordance with the provisions of Article 51 of the Institutional Act,

"1. To accept and to express its appreciation for the invitation because of the reiterated confidence thereby expressed by the Dominican Government in the work of the Commission.

"2. To maintain its office in Santo Domingo, and to go to the Dominican territory, if the circumstances make this advisable, as a complete group or through the sending of a subcommittee, or its Chairman, or members of the Commission individually, representing it.

"3. To continue, in the Dominican Republic, in accordance with the competence established in its Statute, its Regulations, and the practice already observed in that country by the Commission, the defense of the human rights set forth in the American Declaration of the Rights and Duties of Man, and particularly those envisaged in the Second Part of the Institutional Act, *insofar as they coincide with those set forth in the said Declaration,* (italics added) maintaining, in the performance of its functions, the respect due to the personality, sovereignty and independence of that American state."

The Provisional Government was notified by the note of October 19 of the Commission's acceptance of the invitation in the terms stated in this resolution.*

Thus the ground rules were laid for the final stage of

---

* *Report of the Twelfth Session*, Oct. 4-15, 1965—OEA/Ser.L/V/II.13—Doc. 26.

the Commission's work in the Dominican Republic. There had in fact been no gap in its presence as the representation of the Commission had continued during the interval between the replacement of the two Governments by the Provisional Government and the exchange cited above.

Activities of the Commission

With the establishment of headquarters at the Hotel Embajador, the Commission's offices seemed to become the mecca of all the suffering, mistreated, maltreated people in the Dominican Republic. Its doors were open to all and thousands found their way there. At the peak of the flow of petitioners in June and July as many as 100 were interviewed daily. Other complaints came by phone, by mail, from both Governments, from private organizations.

It became apparent immediately that the Commission would have to focus its resources on the area of rights encompassed by life, liberty, and personal security. In fact, the bulk of alleged violations related to the rights of life, to liberty and personal security, including freedom from cruel and inhuman treatment, the right of protection from arbitrary and illegal detention and arrest, and the right to inviolability of the home. The Commission gave attention as it could to violations of the rights of assembly, of freedom of opinion, and expression, and of residence and movement. Denunciations of violations of the latter right came from all sides, with two competing governments occupying territories separated by the Inter-American Peace Force. Invasions and seizures of residences were flagrant and frequent especially in the Constitutionalist Zone. Arbitrary interference with the right of travel within and to and from the country was widespread. It was decided that property damages and interference with property rights, aside from invasions of and damages to the home, would have to wait until a later date.

128

The contrast between the pressures and the needs for assistance and relief, and the resources and powers available to the Commission, was at times almost overwhelming. Yet the people did not despair; they continued to come. One felt at times that the Commission's principal or most useful function was a psychiatric one of extending therapeutic relief to suffering and oppressed people. Never before, or at least not in the memory of most of the petitioners had there been a governmental authority, certainly not an international one, to which they could carry and tell their troubles, with some hope of help. Even if the troubles were often beyond the reach of the Commission, the law of coincidence was on its side, for with the gradual relaxation of tensions, relief came often enough to maintain the credit of the Commission with its endless line of clients.

But there were legal guarantees to be invoked, as both Governments had undertaken to respect and to enforce the human rights established in the American Declaration of the Rights and Duties of Man and to accord to the Commission all the "facilities essential for the proper fulfillment of its mission". Even in the abnormal situation of an uneasy truce and barely concealed civil war, the two governments were not immune to repeated representations, reiterated pressures, constant scrutiny of all their violations, and to publicity. And the Commission made persistent and steady use of these tools, the only effective instruments of power and coercion at its disposal.

Thousands were arrested and held in prison, the bulk of them political prisoners held without cause and seldom informed of charges or given a hearing. The conditions in the prisons, never up to modern standards with the hangover from Trujillo's truly medieval methods, became intolerable under the pressure of the mass arrests of the early days of the revolution. Brutal and inhuman treatment, while contrary to the rules, at least after the advent of the Commission, were charged and proved in too many cases. There were many charges of drumhead executions; many people in the revolutionary confusion disappeared, with distracted relatives searching fruitlessly for them.

The Commission concentrated its energies in trying to bring about an alleviation of these conditions. It gave urgent attention to all charges of imminent executions, and to the investigation of murders, assassinations and missing persons. The latter was a source of continuing frustration. The Commission was instrumental in bringing about the appointment by Secretary General Mora of a group of criminologists who carried out a thorough and dramatic investigation of the Hacienda Haras case, involving charges of executions by night by forces of the Government of National Reconstruction in the early days of the fighting.

The criminologists concluded that:

"First—the bodies . . . were those of persons who had been killed by wounds caused by firearms, after being detained and carried to the site (on the Hacienda Haras) where they were shot and abandoned unburied.

"Second—All the places where the bodies were found were situated in that part of the territory of the Dominican Republic controlled by the Government of National Reconstruction.

"Third—Persuasive indications exist for attributing the detentions, the transfer of the prisoners and the executions to police and military elements.

"Fourth—The executions in question had been carried out most probably at night.

"Fifth—It is improbable that the authorities were ignorant of these tragic events.

"Sixth—The circumstances that actions essentially similar were carried out in widely separated places, is cause for believing not only in their military origin but in an established policy of prosecuting the elimination of adversaries, executing them precipitately without trial, and leaving the bodies abandoned, so that the fate of the victims would serve as a lesson and an exemplary warning to the people."*

The Commission repeatedly visited all the principal prisons in the Santo Domingo area and most of those in the interior. It kept up a steady pressure for release of prisoners against whom no charges had been filed, or for proper hearings and trials, for improved food, sanitary and medical facilities and treatment of the ill. It interviewed prisoners, checked lists, searched for missing persons, and inspected cells and prison facilities. It was denied access in only two places, once at the San Isidro Air Base and twice at the military prison in the Province of San Francisco de Nacoris. In the latter place the prison commandant was replaced shortly thereafter and a new provincial governor installed. In general the Commission was well received and given adequate cooperation in carrying out its mission.

The Commission made it a general practice to visit promptly, so far as its limited manpower permitted, the scene of all alleged atrocities and major violations to gather information and reassure the victims. It travelled freely in its own car, unescorted, throughout both zones of the city and throughout the country. This was accomplished without incident and with a uniformly friendly reception. One report of an attempt to shoot two officers of the Commission as they were boarding a helicopter at the Inter-American Peace Force landing field adjacent to the hotel turned out to be an indiscriminate sniping attempt

---

* OEA, *Tenth Meeting of Consultation*, Doc. 231, July 11, 1965.

to disable the machine. The Commission's own flag, designed by its Executive Secretary, displayed on the car was a passport for entry anywhere at any time.

The Commission's effort was to maintain a steady pressure on the authorities of both Governments to maintain normal order to the extent possible under the disturbed and abnormal conditions, and to repress and punish excesses and violations by military, police, and other government personnel. It maintained continuous contact with top officials of each government from the President down, with military and police commanders, with the Procurador General and with prison commandants. It maintained a continuous stream of written representations and information through the Ministers of Foreign Affairs, and where appropriate to other officials, on all violations reported to or discovered by it. It maintained a steady follow-up on these representations.

Conditions in the prisons, while falling much short of normal modern standards, as noted above, gradually improved with a decrease in crowding after the opening weeks. While no complete data was available as to the number of political prisoners, the Commission estimated they numbered more than 4000 at the beginning of June, a number gradually reduced as the work of the Commission progressed. An Investigating and Review Board (Junta Depuradora) set up by the Government of National Reconstruction at the end of May worked slowly at first and suspended activities at the middle of July. Under pressure from the Commission it was reconstituted on July 27. As of the middle of August the number of political prisoners had been reduced to 350 civilians and 132 military in La Victoria Penitentiary, the principal prison, 50 in the National Police Palace, the second largest prison, 80 at the San Isidro Air Base, and 90 in the interior of the country.

On August 27, 1965 the Representative of the Commission appealed in writing to the Presidents of the two contending Governments for the release of all remaining political prisoners, as a general amnesty was provided in the Institutional Act. This appeal was motivated partly by a widespread fear of the maltreatment or murder, of the military prisoners in particular, before the Provisional Government took over. Both parties agreed to release the military prisoners and on August 31, September 2, and 3, the extraordinary spectacle occurred of the physical transfer of the custody of these prisoners to the Representative of the Inter-American Human Rights Commission. The Constitutionalist Government transferred to his custody at the Fortress Ozana 108 officers and men of the National Police who were transported by buses supplied by the Inter-American Peace Force to the zone of the Government of National Reconstruction. After verifying that the men were in good physical condition the Representative signed a document acknowledging the transfer. In a comparable ceremony at La Victoria Penitentiary 10 officers and 55 men of the army and marine corps were released to the custody of the Commission's Representative by the officials of the Government of National Reconstruction. The Commission also acknowledged in September the release of 18 marines who had been imprisoned on the Isla Beata.

The attitude of both Governments continued after the June 8 and 9 agreements to be generally cooperative, with constant professions of good intentions, but performance falling below promise.

The Provisional President, García Godoy, has given consistent evidence of a desire and intention to enforce the human rights provisions covered by the Institutional Act. Violations have continued to flow from military and police excesses and from the inability of the President in all cases, in the continuing disturbed conditions, to commend the obedience of the diverse forces with which he has to deal. In view of the succession of crimes and acts of violence by military and police personnel as well as private citizens the Representative of the Commission in Santo Domingo issued an appeal to the nation on February 11, 1966. He said that the Provisional President had given a demonstration of his determination to assure respect for human rights as provided in the Institutional Act. The appeal continued:

> "Nevertheless assured respect for these rights depends upon the effective operation of national institutions, especially preventive and repressive action by the police and the judiciary. . .

> "For this reason, the Inter-American Commission on Human Rights exhorts all authorities of the Dominican Republic, within the limits of its authority, to respect and to enforce respect for human rights as defined in the Institutional Act and in international declarations, repressing firmly violations of these rights. It also exhorts the Dominican people of all classes that they cooperate with patriotism and serenity so that it may be possible to establish the rule of law in the country".*

The Law and Practice of the Commission

It is obvious from the foregoing account that the Commission's activities were of a character not literally contemplated in its Statute. It was envisaged there as a body to make studies and reports, "to make recommendations to the Governments of member states in general, if it con-

---

* For a summary of the activities of the Commission during the first three months see *Preliminary Report of the President of the Commission,* OEA/Ser.-L/V./II.12, Doc. 2, June 23, 1965; *Report on the Activities of the Inter-American Commission on Human Rights in the Dominican Republic,* June 1-Aug. 31, 1965. OEA/Ser.L/V/II.3, Doc. 14, Oct. 15, 1965. Other reports of individual members are confidential.

siders such action advisable", to develop an awareness of human rights, to urge the Governments to supply it with information and to serve the OAS as an advisory body.

In the Dominican Republic it found itself literally on the firing line of human rights. It was there in the words of the inviting Governments for the purpose of verifying on the spot "the abuses to which defenseless citizens were being subjected", of verifying and adopting the pertinent measures with regard to "abuses and assassinations" and of making on the spot examination of the general situation with regard to human rights. Both parties, as previously noted, agreed to provide the Commission with "all of the facilities essential for the proper fulfillment of its mission". This mission was clearly not regarded as one of studying and reporting but of using its resources and prestige to help to bring an end to the excesses and the violations of human rights. Under the Institutional Act (Art. 51), calling for the continued presence of the Commission until the installation of the elected Government, the Provisional Government promised to cooperate with the Commission to enable it "to observe the fulfillment" of the guarantees of human rights contained in Part II of the Act. To observe seems clearly to have been intended to include action to help assure compliance.

The Commission was thus continuously confronted with the dilemma of reconciling what it was doing with what it is authorized to do under its Statute. This it sought to accomplish by basing its action on the authority of the Statute and not on the action documents of the two Governments and the Institutional Act. Thus in the Resolution of October 15, 1965, adopted at its Twelfth Session (quoted above), accepting the invitation of the Provisional Government pursuant to the Institutional Act, the Commission declared its determination to proceed "in accordance with the competence embodied in its Statute, its Regulations and the practice observed by the Commission".

Fortunately the Commission, as previously pointed out, had laid a foundation for its activities by interpreting Article 9b of its Statute as empowering it "to make general recommendations to each individual member state as well as to all of them". It combined this with an assertion of the right to review conditions in individual countries where flagrant and persistent violations of human rights obtain and to make recommendations concerning them. Consequently it was not too much of a distortion to treat the Commission's continuing representations to the Dominican authorities as recommendations falling within this interpretation and practice. Nevertheless, it is necessary to recognize with candor that its Dominican experience marked the culmination of the transition of the Commission from a study and reporting body to one with far broader action range and role than ever anticipated by its creators.

In this it has moved much beyond the role played by the United Nations Commission on Human Rights, and even beyond or different from that enjoyed by the European Human Rights Commission. The latter has jurisdiction over individual complaints, within carefully prescribed rules, but it has never played a part with respect to individual Governments such as that now exercised by the Inter-American Commission. The United Nations Commission has approached both the question of individual complaints and of recommendations to individual governments with great caution and restraint.

In view of the vociferous criticism of the United States and of the Organization of American States on the grounds of improper intervention, the attitude thus displayed toward the activities of the Inter-American Human Rights Commission in support of human rights in the Dominican Republic is a political phenomenon of unique significance.

Expansion of the Commission's Competence

That the broad view taken by the Commission of its proper role and competence has the general support of the American States is demonstrated by the action taken by the Second Special Inter-American Conference at Rio last November.

From the beginning of its existence the Commission has been restive under what it has characterized as its limited competence. What has irked the Commission most is its lack of jurisdiction over individual complaints. However, as we have seen, under its interpretation of its Statute, the the Commission has in fact exercised an even broader competence relative to patterns of general violations of human rights by Member states, by asserting the right to make reports with findings and recommendations concerning the behavior of individual Member states.

In the preparation of the Statute, the Council had decided after prolonged debate and a sharp division of opinion, not to confer upon the Commission jurisdiction in individual cases. Nevertheless, after canvassing the matter at great length in its first session, the Commission recommended to the Council of the OAS amendments to the Statute conferring jurisdiction on it to examine complaints by individuals, groups or associations of "serions violations of human rights as defined in the American Declaration", to make recommendations to the Governments concerned, and to publish reports in such cases "if the governments accused of the acts examined by the Commission fail to adopt the recommended measures within a reasonable time".*

As the Council had failed to take action on this proposal the Commission took advantage of the Second Special Conference to make a modified recommendation that it be

---

* *Report on Work of First Session*, Oct. 3-28, 1960, OEA/Ser.L/V/II.1, Doc. 32.

given jurisdiction in individual cases falling within a selected group of political and civil rights.*

In the Preamble to its Resolution XXII, entitled "Expanded Functions of the Inter-American Commission on Human Rights", the Special Conference declared that the Commission had performed valuable service in carrying out its mandate and asserted the agreement of the member states that it should be strengthened by broadening its responsibilities in an effort to promote greater respect for human rights in the hemisphere. The Conference then resolved:

"1. To request the Inter-American Commission on Human Rights to conduct a continuing survey of the observance of fundamental human rights in each of the member states of the Organization.

"2. To request the Commission to give particular attention in this survey to observance of the human rights referred to in articles I, II, III, IV, XVIII, XXV, and XXVI of the American Declaration of the Rights and Duties of Man."**

"3. To authorize the Commission to examine communications submitted to it and any other available information, so that it may address to the government of any American state a request for information deemed pertinent by the Commission, and so that it may make recommendations, when it deems this appropriate, with the objective of bringing about more effective observance of fundamental human rights.

---

* *Report Submitted by the Inter-American Commission on Human Rights,* OEA/Ser.L/V/II.11, Doc. 5, Oct. 1965.

** The Articles listed are: I. Life, liberty, and personal security; II. Equality before the law; III. Religious freedom and worship; IV. Freedom of investigation, opinion, expression and dissemination; XVIII, A fair trial; XXV, Protection from arbitrary arrest; XXVI, Due process of law.

"4. To request the Commission to submit a report annually to the Inter-American Conference or Meeting of Consultation of Ministers of Foreign Affairs. This report should include statement of progress achieved in realization of the goals set forth in the American Declaration, a statement of areas in which further steps are needed to give effect to the human rights set forth in the American Declaration, and such observations as the Commission may deem appropriate on matters covered in the communications submitted to it and in other information available to the Commission."*

Although somewhat veiled in its language, as is not unusual in OAS Conference practice, these provisions do two things— (1) They spell out, in effect, the practice which the Commission has been following under its interpretation of Article 9b of its Statute, as previously described; and (2) they authorize the Commission to examine communications, and make requests for pertinent information and appropriate recommendation "to the government of any American state", without any limitation as to whether this is done collectively or individually. Thus the Commission appears to have achieved the long coveted authority to examine and make recommendations on individual complaints. This is subject to the limitation, stated in paragraph 5, that in exercising the functions set forth in paragraphs 3 and 4, the Commission "shall verify, as a condition precedent, whether the internal legal procedure and remedies of a member state have been duly adjudicated and exhausted". Only practice can tell what the consequences of this limitation may be.

A Special Committee composed of representatives of

---

* *Final Act of the Second Special Inter-American Conference,* November 30, 1965. OEA/Ser.E XIII.1.

each of the members of the OAS, charged by the Special Conference with the preparation of the draft Charter Amendments projected in the Final Act of Rio, has recently completed its work in Panama. Among the draft amendments agreed upon is the one raising the Commission on Human Rights to Charter status. It provides: "There shall be an Inter-American Commission on Human Rights which shall have, among other functions, that of promoting the observance and defense of human rights." The structure, competence, and procedure of the Commission is to be determined in an Inter-American Convention on Human Rights. Under another action of the Rio Conference the Convention on Human Rights drafted at Santiago in 1959 and draft Conventions proposed by Chile and Uruguay are to be examined and amended within a year by the Council of the OAS, with the advice of the present Commission on Human Rights, and submitted to a Special Conference. Until the entrance into force of that Convention the present Commission under a transitory provision of the amended Charter, would continue to carry on its responsibility for keeping vigilance over the observance of human rights within the Inter-American system.*

It is not possible within the scope of this paper to develop the implications of these rather complex legal provisions. Nevertheless, it is necessary to take account of their formulation and adoption by the American States in evaluating the work of the Human Rights Commission in the Dominican Republic. For what these provisions accomplish by implication, if not explicitly, is an endorsement of the measures and methods utilized by the Commission in the discharge of its mandate to promote the observance of and respect for human rights in the Dominican Republic.

---

* *Final Act of the Special Committee*, OEA/Ser.K/XIII/1.1, Doc. 90, April 1, 1966.

This represents a substantial step beyond anything ever undertaken before, through action by an international agency in support of human rights, either in the Organization of American States or in any other international organization.

Selected Bibliography on the Dominican Republic Crisis*

DOCUMENTARY SOURCES

Alfaro, Ricardo J. Memorandum (question of defining aggression). 1951 V.2 Yb. Int'l L. Comm'n 33—40.

American foreign ministers condemn Sino-Soviet intervention in American states: three statements by Secretary Herter at the seventh meeting of consultation of the American foreign ministers at San José, Costa Rica; together with the text of a declaration adopted . . . Aug. 28, 1960. . . . Sept. 12, 1960. 43 Dep't State Bull. 395—409.

Assessment of the situation on the Dominican Republic; statement June 17, 1965, Lyndon B. Johnson. 1965. 53 Dep't State Bull. 19—21.

Charter of Punta del Este (in U.S. Administrative law. Legislation on foreign relations with explanatory notes. Washington, 1962, pp.543—55).

Dominican crisis ended; with text of act of Dominican reconciliation. 1965. 17 Américas 41—42.

Dominican Republic: act of Dominican reconciliation and institutional act (signed at Santo Domingo Aug. 31, 1965). Nov. 1965. 4 Int'l Leg. Materials 1150—70.

Dominican Republic. Here is our answer; a summary of the comments of the government of the Dominican Republic on June 6, 1960; report of the Inter-American peace committee. Ciudad Trujillo. 1960. 25p.

The Dominican situation. Aug. 1965. 1 (1) OAS Chronicle 1—11.

Documents on the Dominican Republic. 1962. Docs. Am. For. Relations 461—63; 1963:392—97.

Harvard Law School, Research in International Law. The law of responsibility of states for damage done in their territory to the person or property of foreigners (draft convention). 1929. Am. J. Int'l L. (Supp.) 133—218.

Inter-American Juridical Committee. Opinion on the scope of the powers of the council of the Organization of American states. March 1961. 21p. (mimeo) (OAS/SER.I/VI.2)

Inter-American Commission on Human Rights.
Report on the situation regarding human rights in the Dominican Republic. May 22, 1962. 79p. (OEA/Ser.L/V/II.4),

---

* Prepared by the Reference Librarian of the Association of the Bar

Report on the work accomplished during the eleventh session (special), July 21—23, 1965. (OEA/Ser.L/V/II.12, Doc 10, 1965).

Protection of human rights in the face of suspension of guaranties or state of siege; observations and comments prepared by the secretariat. Washington, Pan-American Union. 1964. 8p.

Inter-American Conference for the Maintenance of Continental Peace and Security, Rio de Janeiro 1947.

Inter-American Conference for the maintenance of continental peace and security, Rio de Janeiro, Brazil . . . Washington, Pan American Union. 1946. 142p.

Inter-American treaty of reciprocal assistance between the United States of America and other American Republics . . . proclaimed by the President of the United States of America Dec. 9, 1948, entered into force Dec. 3, 1948. Washington, Gov't Print. Off. 1949. 40p.

Inter-American conference for the maintenance of continental peace and security, Rio de Janeiro, Aug. 15—Sept. 2, 1947. Washington. 1960. 7p. (Eng. OEA/Ser./A/1)

Inter-American Conference, 11th, Quito, 1961. General Secretariat. Latin-américa y el derecho internacional americano. 1959. 150p.

Inter-American Council of Jurists.

Inter-American court to protect the rights of man. Washington, Dep't of Int'l Law, Pan American Union. 1953. 19p.

Recognition of de facto governments. Washington, Dep't of Int'l Law, Pan American Union. 1953. 75p.

Inter-American Council of Jurists-American Judicial Committee.

Contribution of the American continent to the principles of international law that govern the responsibility of the state. Opinion prepared in accordance with res. VI of the Tenth interamerican conference. . . . Washington, Pan American Union. 1962. 127p. (OEA/Ser.I/VI 2)

Instrument relating to violations of the principles of non-intervention. Draft and report in accordance with res. VII, fifth meeting of consultation. Washington, Pan American Union. 1959. 29p.

Opinion on the legal aspects of the draft declaration on non-intervention presented by the Mexican delegation. Prepared in accordance with res. V, fifth meeting of consultation. Washington, Pan American Union. 1961. 29p.

Opinion on the scope of the powers of the Council of the Organization of American states. Prepared in accordance with resolution of April 21, 1949 . . . and with res. III, 1st meeting of consultation. Washington, Pan American Union, 1961. 21p.

Study . . . of the proposal of Ecuador concerning the Inter-American peace committee (chap. 1, topic 4c of the agenda). Washington, Pan American Union. 1960. 11p.

Study on the juridical relationship between respect for human rights and the exercise of democracy. Washington, Pan American Union. 1960. 35p. (CIJ—52 (English).

Inter-American Peace Committee. Report to the eighth meeting of consultation of ministers of foreign affairs. Washington, Pan American Union. 1962. v.p. (OEA/Ser.L/III/CIP/1/62 (English).

Johnson, Lyndon B.
The Dominican Republic—a target of tyranny. 1965. 31 Vital Speeches 450—52.

Statement on Dominican Republic, May 2, 1965. May 7, 1965. 23 Cong. Q. W. Rep. 881—82.

Mann, Thomas C. The Dominican crisis: correcting some misconceptions. 1965. 53 Dep't State Bull. 730—38.

Manning, William Ray. Diplomatic correspondence of the United States concerning the independence of the Latin American nations; selected and arranged. New York, Oxford Univ. Press. 1925. 3v.

Martin, E. M. Interdependence and the principles of self-determination and nonintervention. 1963. 48 Dep't State Bull. 710—15.

Meeker, L. C. The Dominican situation in perspective of international law. 1965. 53 Dep't State Bull. 60—65.

Miller, Edward G., jr. Nonintervention and collective responsibility in the Americas. 1950. 22 Dep't State Bull. 768—70.

OAS achieves reconciliation in Dominican Republic. 1965. 53 Dep't State Bull. 477—80.

OAS in action; OAS continues efforts in Dominican Republic. June 1965. 17 Américas 42—44.

OAS foreign ministers provide for establishment of interamerican force in Dominican Republic. 1965. 52 Dep't State Bull. 854—68.

Organization of American States. Charter. Charter of the Organization of American States signed at Bogotá, April 30, 1948 . . . proclaimed by the President of the United States of America, Dec. 27, 1951, entered into force Dec. 13, 1951. Washington, Gov't Print. Off. 1952. 95p.

Organization of American States. Council.
Protocol to the convention on duties and rights of states in the event of civil strife. Washington, Pan American Union. 1953. 30p.

Regulations of the meeting of consultation of ministers of foreign affairs. Approved by the council . . . March 1, 1950. The

145

temporary provisions applicable to the seventh meeting . . . were approved . . . Aug. 8, 1960. Washington, Pan American Union. 1960. 6p. (OEA/Ser.F./I.1).

Regulations of the meeting of consultation of ministers of foreign affairs, to serve as organ of consultation in application of the inter-American treaty of reciprocal assistance. Washington, Pan American Union. 1960. 10p. (OEA/Ser.F./I.2 (English) JX 1980.356.A231.

Organization of American States.

Fifth meeting of consultation of ministers of foreign affairs. Santiago, Chile, Aug. 12—18, 1959: final act. Washington, Pan American Union. 1960. OEA/Ser.C./II.5).

Eighth meeting of consultation of ministers of foreign affairs, Punta del Este, Uruguay, Jan. 22—31, 1962: final act. Washington, Pan American Union. 1962. 20p. (OEA/Ser.C./II.8).

First report of the special committee of the tenth meeting of consultation of ministers of foreign affairs of the American states, submitted at the fourth plenary session held on May 7—8, 1965. May 8, 1965. 20p. (OEA/Ser.F./II.10) Also issued as U.N. Doc. S/6364, May 18, 1965.

Tenth meeting of consultation of ministers of foreign affairs: establishment of inter-American force in Dominican Republic. Resolution adopted in the third plenary session held on May 6, 1965. 4 Int'l Leg. Materials 596—94.

Resolutions of the tenth inter-American conference, Caracas, Venezuela, 1—28 March 1954 (on human rights). 1954 Yb. on Human Rights 394—95.

Report of special committee on the Dominican Republic. 1965. 4 Int'l Leg. Materials 557—76.

Pan American Union.

Act of Dominican reconciliation and institutional act. (OEA/Ser.F./II.10, Doc. 363, 7 Sept. 1965).

Conseje de la organización de los estados americanos. Acta de la sesión extraordinaria . . . 29 April 1965. (OEA/Ser.G./II, C-a-569 (aprobada) Parte II29, April 1965).

Decima reunión de consulta de ministres de relaciones exteriores (OEA/Ser.F./II.10, June 8, 1965).

Documentos oficiales de la organización de los estados americanos: indices y lista general. Vol. 1—1960—. Washington. 1961—.

Final act, second special inter-American conference, Rio de Janeiro, Brazil, Nov. 17—30, 1965. Resolution XXII, "expanded functions of the Inter-American commission on human rights." (OEA/Ser.C./I.13, 1965).

Inter-American conference for the maintenance of continental peace and security, Rio de Janeiro, Aug. 15—Sept. 2, 1947. Report on the results of the conference . . . Washington. 1947. 83p.

Manual of inter-American relations; a systematic classification of the treaties, conventions, resolutions adopted at the inter-American conference. 1956. Conf. Ser. 42. 344p.

Pan American Union. Department of Legal Affairs.
Human rights in the American states. Preliminary edition. Nov. 1960. 226p.

Inter-American treaties and conventions, signatures, ratifications and deposits with explanatory notes. Rev. ed. Washington. 1961. (Treaty ser. no.9).

Inter-American treaty of reciprocal assistance, applications. Washington. 1964. 2v (V.1, 1948—59; V.2, 1960—64)

The Organization of American states and the United Nations. Manuel Canyes. 1960. 63p.

Pan American Union. Inter-American Juridical Committee. Study on the juridical relationship between respect for human rights and the exercise of democracy. May 1960. 35p. (mimeo).

Pilmpton, Francis T.P. Principles of international law concerning friendly relations and cooperation among states. 1964. 50 Dep't State Bull. 133—43.

Report from Santo Domingo: ad hoc committee. Nov. 1965. 17 Américas 43.

Rusk, Dean. OAS to help restore democratic order in Dominican Republic, statement June 2, 1965 with text of resolution June 21, 1965. 52 Dep't State Bull. 1017—18.

Security council authorizes U.N. representative in Dominican Republic. 1965. 52 Dep't State Bull. 869—85.

United Nations. Secretariat. Department of Social Affairs. Yearbook on human rights 1946—. (annual)

United Nations. Security council considers situation in Dominican Republic; statements, May 19—21, 1965, Adlai E. Stevenson. 1965. 52 Dep't State Bull. 913—19.

U.S. acts to meet threat in Dominican Republic. 1965. 52 Dep't State Bull. 738—47.

U.S. Congress. House. Comm. on Foreign Affairs.
(87.2) Regional and other documents concerning United States relations with Latin America. Washington. 1962. 204p.

(89.1) Communism in Latin America. Hearings . . . Feb. 16, 25, March 2, 10, 16, 30, 1965. Washington, Gov't Print. Off. 1965. 123p.

(89.1) International communism in the western hemisphere.

Hearings . . . on H.Res.542 (H. Res. 560) . . . Washington, Gov't Print. Off. 1965. 43p.

(89.1) Sense of the House of representatives relative to international communism in the western hemisphere. Report no. 983 to accompany H.Res.560. Washington, Gov't Print. Off. 1965. 3p.

U.S. Congress. Senate. Comm. on the Judiciary.
Documentation of communist penetration in Latin America. Washington, Gov't Print. Off. 1965. 392p.

(89.1) Testimony of Elias Wessin y Wessin, hearing before subcom. to investigate administration of internal security act and other internal security laws, Oct. 1, 1965. Washington, Gov't Print. Off. 1965. V. + 107—275.

U.S. Congress. Senate. Comm. on Foreign Relations.
(81.1) A decade of American foreign policy; basic documents 1941—49. Washington. 1950. (Sen. doc. 123) Part V, The inter-American system, pp.411—53.

(86.1) United States-Latin American relations: the Organization of American states. 1959. 87p. (Prepared by Northwestern univ.)

Background information relating to the Dominican Republic. Washington, Gov't Print. Off. 1965. 100p.

U.S. Department of State. Right to protect citizens in foreign countries by landing forces. Memorandum of the solicitor for the Department of state, Oct. 5, 1912. 3d rev. ed. w/supplemented appendix up to 1933. Washington, Gov't Print Off. 1934. 130p.

U.S. Department of State. Bureau of Public Affairs. The Dominican crisis . . . the hemisphere acts. Washington, Gov't Print. Off. 1965. (Dep't of State pub.7971, Inter-American series 92)

U.S. submits to U.N. security council OAS documents on Dominican Republic; statement June 18, 1965 with texts of documents, Adlai E. Stevenson. 1965. 53 Dep't State Bull. 132—35.

BOOKS AND PAMPHLETS

General

American Assembly. The United States and Latin America; background papers and the final report of the sixteenth assembly. Arden House, Harriman, N.Y., Oct. 15—18, 1959. Final ed. New York. 1959. 221p.

Arciniegas, Germán. Caribbean: sea of the new world; trans. from the Spanish by Harriet de Onís. New York. Knopf. 1946. 464p.

Barber, Willard F. and Ronning, C. Neale. Internal security and military power: counterinsurgency and civic action in Latin America. Columbus, Ohio State Univ. Press. 1966. 384p.

Berle, Adolf A., jr. Latin America; diplomacy and reality. New York, Harper & Row (for the Council on Foreign Relations). 1962. 144p.

Blakeslee, George Hubbard, ed. Mexico and the Caribbean. New York, G. E. Stechert. 1920. 363p.

Bosch, Juan. Unfinished experiment, democracy in the Dominican Republic. New York, Praeger. 1965. 239p.

Caicedo Castilla, José Joaquín. El panamericanismo. Buenos Aires, R. Depalma. 1961. 484p.

Dominican chaos, by the editors of Deadline data on world affairs. New York, Keynote Pubs. 1965. 51p. (On Record, v.2, no.10)

Dozer, Donald Marquand. Are we good neighbors? Three decades of inter-American relations 1930—60. Gainesville, Univ. of Florida Press. 1959.

Draper, Theodore. Dominican debacle. New York, Viking Press. 1966.

Goldwert, Marvin. The constabulary in the Dominican Republic and Nicaragua: progeny and legacy of United States intervention. Gainesville, Univ. of Florida Press. 1962. 55p.

Halpern, Manfred. The morality and politics of intervention. New York, Council on Religion and International Affairs. 1963. 36p. (Also in Rosenau, James N. International aspects of civil strife. Princeton, Princeton Univ. Press. 1964. pp.249—88)

Kurzman, Dan. Santo Domingo: revolt of the damned. New York, Putnam. 1965. 310p.

Lieuwen, Edwin.

Arms and politics in Latin America. Rev. ed. New York, Praeger (for the Council on Foreign Relations). 1961. 335p.

Generals vs. presidents; neomilitarism in Latin America. New York, Praeger. 1965. 160p.

U.S. policy in Latin America; a short history. New York Praeger. 1965.

Mallin, J. Caribbean crisis. New York, Doubleday. 1965. 101p.

Manger, William. Pan America in crisis; the future of the OAS. With an introd. by Alberto Lleras Camargo and foreward by Hector David Castro. Washington, Public Affairs Press. 1961. 104p.

Mecham, J. Lloyd. A survey of United States-Latin American relations. Boston, Houghton Mifflin. 1965. 487p.

Munro, D. G. Intervention and dollar diplomacy in the Caribbean 1900—21. Princeton, Princeton Univ. Press. 1964. 553p.

149

Ortiz de Zevallos, Javier. América frente a la intervención colectiva auspicida. Lima. 1947. 91p.

✓ Palmer, Thomas Waverly. Search for a Latin America policy. Gainesville, Univ. of Florida Press. 1957. 217p.

✓ Perkins, Dexter. The United States and Latin America. Baton Rouge, Louisiana State Univ. Press. 1961. 124p.

Porter, Charles O. The struggle for democracy in Latin America. New York, Macmillan. 1961. 215p.

Prada, Jaime Luz Marina. Paralelo entre la ONU y OEA; solución pacifica de las controversias. Bogotá. 1960. 93p.

✓ Rodman, Selden. Quisqueya: a history of the Dominican Republic. Seattle, Univ. of Washington Press. 1964. 202p.

Schmitt, Karl M. and Burks, David D. Evolution or chaos: dynamics of Latin American government and politics. New York, Praeger. 1963. 308p.

Stuart, Graham Henry. Latin America and the United States. 3d ed. New York, London, D. Appleton-Century. 1938. 510p.

✓ Szulc, Ted.
Dominican diary. New York, Delocorte. 1965. 306p.
The winds of revolution. Latin America today and tomorrow. New York, Praeger. 1962. 300p.

Tannenbaum, Frank.
The American tradition in foreign policy. Norman, Univ. of Oklahoma press. 1955. 178p.
Ten keys to Latin America. New York, Knopf. 1962. 237p.

Walker, Stanley. Journey toward the sunlight; a story of the Dominican Republic and its people. New York, Caribbean Library. 1947. 226p.

Welles, Sumner. Naboth's vineyard; the Dominican Republic 1844—1924. New York, Payson & Clarke, Ltd. 1928. 2v.

Whitaker, Arthur P.
Las Américas y un mundo en crisis. Traducción de Ernesto Montenegro. Lancaster, Pa., Lancaster Press. 1946. 366p.
Development of American regionalism; the Organization of American states. March 1951. 469 Int'l Conciliation 121—64.
The western hemisphere: its rise and decline. Ithaca, Cornell Univ. Press. 1954. 194p.

✓ Wythe, George. The United States and inter-American relations: a contemporary appraisal. Gainesville, Univ. of Florida Press. 1964. 251p.

Zanotti, Isidro. Organizacao des estados americanos. Rio de Janeiro. 1948. 104p.

Legal

Alvarado Garaicoa, Teodoro. Los principios internacionales de no intervención y autodeterminación. La Haya, Dijkman. 1962. 78p.

Alvarado, Rafael, ed. Los principales instrumentos; sintesis de derecho internacional americano. Compilación y notas. Quito, Casa de la Cultura Ecuatoriana. 1960. 172p.

Bayona Ortiz, Antonio. Aspectos políticos—jurídicos de la organización internacional americana. Bogotá, Impr. del. Departamento. 1953. 131p.

Blackman, Henry M. United States policy and the inter-American peace system, 1889—1952. Paris. 1952. 221p.

Borchard, Edwin M. The diplomatic protection of citizens abroad. New York, Banks Law Pub. Co. 1915. 988p.

Bowett, D. W. United Nations forces: a legal study. New York, Praeger. 1964. 579p.

Brownlie, Ian. International law and the use of force by states. Oxford, Clarendon Press. 1963. 532p.

√Burke, William T. The legal regulation of minor international coercion: a framework of inquiry (in Stanger, R. J., ed. Essays on intervention. Columbus, Ohio state univ. press, 1964, pp.87—125)

Canyes Santacana, Manuel. The Organization of American states and the United Nations. 5th ed. Washington, Pan American Union. 1960. 63p.

Cardozo, Michael H. Intervention: benefaction as justification (in Stanger, R. J., ed. Essays on Intervention. Columbus, Ohio state univ. press, 1964, pp.63—85)

Cheng, Bin. General principles of law, as applied by international courts and tribunals; with a foreword by Georg Schwarzenberger. London, Stevens. 1953. 490p.

Dreier, John C. The Organization of American states and the hemisphere crisis. New York, Harper & Row (for the Council on Foreign Relations). 1962.

Fabela, Isidro. Intervención. Mexico, Escuela Nacional de Ciencias Politicas y Sociales. 1959. 376p.

Facio, Gonzalo J. El reconocimiento como institución jurídica americana al servico de la democracia. San José, Impr. Falco. 1952, 24p.

Falk, Richard A.

Janus tormented: the international law of internal war (in Rosenau, James N. International aspects of civil strife. Princeton, Princeton univ. press, 1964, pp.185—248)

The legitimacy of legislative intervention by the United Nations

151

(in Stanger, R. J., ed. Essays on intervention. Columbus, Ohio state univ. press, 1964, pp.31—61)

Fawcett, J. E. S. Intervention in international law; a study of some recent cases. 1961. 103 Recueil des Cours, V.2, 347—21.

Fenwick, Charles G.
The inter-American system of collective security. 1960. 8 Acad. Inter-Americana de Derecho Comparado e Internacional Curos Monográficos 57—100.

International law. 4th ed. New York, Appleton-Century-Crofts. 1965. pp.285—92.

The Organization of American states; the inter-American regional system. Washington. 1963. 601p.

Fernández-Shaw, Félix G. La organización de los estados americanos. Madrid, Ediciones Cultura Hispánica. 1959. 770p.

Fisher, Roger. Intervention: three problems of policy and law (in Stanger, R. J., ed. Essays on intervention. Columbus, Ohio state univ. press, 1964, pp.3—30)

Fitzmaurice, Gerald. The general principles of international law considered from the standpoint of the rule of law. 1957. 92 Recueil des Cours 1—227.

Freeman, Alwyn V. The political powers of the OAS council (in Lipsky, George A., ed. Law and politics in the world community. Berkeley, Univ. of California press, 1953, pp.252—78)

Ganji, Manouchehr. International protection of human rights. Genève, E. Droz. 1962. 317p.

Garcia-Arias, L. La intervención internacional par causa de humanidad (in Festschrift für Jean Spiropoulos, 1957, pp.163—)

Georgetown University. Institute of World Polity. The law of limited international conflict, a study by the Institute of world polity, Edmund A. Walsh school of foreign service, Georgetown University. Washington, D.C. 1965. 258p.

Gomez Valle, Sara. La no intervención en los estados americanos. Mexico. 1949. 70p.

ᐰ Graber, Doris A. Crisis diplomacy; a history of U.S. intervention policies and practices. Washington, Public Affairs Press. 1959. 402p.

Gross, Leo. States as organs of international law and the problem of auto-interpretation (in Lipsky, George A., ed. Law and politics in the world community. Berkeley, Univ. of California press, 1953, pp. 59—88)

Gilmour, David R. Intervention under the United Nations charter. (Thesis for Ph.D., Edinburgh university, in preparation)

Guillén Atienza, Luis. El principio de no intervención y las doctrinas americas. Santiago de Chile. 1949. 223p. (Colección de estudios de derecho internacional, v.7)

Hackworth, Green Haywood. Digest of international law. Washington, Gov't Print. Off. 1940—44. 8v.

Haedrich, Heinz. Intervention (in Strupp, Karl. Worterbuch des völkerrechts. Berlin, Verlag Walter de Gruyter, 1961, v.2, pp. 144—46)

Hammarskjöld Forums, New York. The Inter-American security system and the Cuban crisis. Background papers and proceedings of the third Hammarskjöld forum. Covey Oliver, author of the working paper. Lyman M. Tondel, jr., ed. Dobbs Ferry, N.Y., Pub. for The Association of the Bar of the City of New York by Oceana. 1965. 96p.

Higgins, Rosalyn. The development of international law through the political organs of the United Nations. London, New York, Oxford Univ. Press. 1963. 402p.

Hoyo Algara, Francisco del. Estudio de la organización de los estados americanos. Mexico. 1952. 108p.

Hughes, Charles Evans. Pan American peace plans. New Haven, Yale Univ. Press. 1929. 68p.

Hyde, Charles Cheney. International law chiefly as interpreted and applied by the United States . . . 2d rev. ed. Boston, Little Brown. 1945. (Intervention, V.1, pp.245—81)

Jasper, Marcel-H. La doctrine de l'intervention chez Grotius, Vattel et Puffendorf. 1932. 38 Rev. de l'Univ. de Bruxelles 59—77.

Jessup, Philip C. A modern law of nations. New York, Macmillan. 1948. 236p.

✓ Kaplan, Morton A. Intervention in internal war: some systematic sources (in Rosenmau, James N. International aspects of civil strife. Princeton, Princeton univ. press, 1964, pp.92—121)

Kelsen, Hans. The law of the United Nations; a critical analysis of its fundamental problems. London, Stevens. 1950. 903p.

—Recent trends in the law of the United Nations, a supplement. New York, Praeger. 1950. pp.909—94.

Lauterpacht, Hersh. The international protection of human rights. 1947. 70 Recueil des Cours 1-108.

López-Jiminez, Ramón. El principio de no intervención en América y la nota Uruguaya. Buenos Aires, Depalma. 1947.

McDougal, Myres and Feliciano, Florentino P. Law and minimum world order; the legal regulation and international coercion. New Haven, Yale Univ. Press. 1961. 872p.

Maúrtua, Victor Manuel. Intervención-conciliación-arbitraje en las conferencias de la Habana, 1928 y Washington, 1929. Habana, Impr. Molina y Cía. 1929. 196p.

153

Mecham, John Lloyd. The United States and inter-American security, 1889—1960. Austin, Univ. of Texas Press. 1961. 514p.

Modelski, George.
The international relations of internal war (in Rosenau, James N., ed. International aspects of civil strife. Princeton, Princeton univ. press, 1964, pp.14—44)
International settlement of internal war (in Rosenau, James N., ed. International aspects of civil strife. Princeton, Princeton univ. press, 1964, pp.122—53)

Moskowitz, Moses. Human rights and world order. Dobbs Ferry, N.Y., Oceana. 1958. 239p.

Munguia Araújo, Carlos N. Intervención. León, Nicaragua. 1945. 56p.

Nawaz, M. K. Intervention by invitation and the U.N. charter. New Delhi. 1959. 7p.

O'Connell, D.P. International law. London, Stevens; Dobbs Ferry, N.Y., Oceana. 1965. V.1, pp.319—48; V.2, pp.1019—31.

Oppenheim, L. F. L. International law: a treatise. 8th ed. by H. Lauterpacht. London, Longmans, Green. 1955. (V.1, Intervention pp.304—20)

Parry, Clive. Some considerations upon the protection of individuals in international law. 1956. 90 Recueil des Cours 657—726.

Potter, Pitman B. L'intervention en droit international moderne. 1930. 32 Recueil des Cours 611—87.

Preuss, Lawrence. Article 2, paragraph 7 of the charter of the United Nations and matters of domestic jurisdiction. 1949. 74 Recueil des Cours 553—652.

Rojas, Galdames René. Organización de los estados americanos. Santiago, Editorial Jurídica de Chile. 1951. pp.396—436.

Ronning, C. Neale.
Law and politics in inter-American diplomacy. New York, Wiley, 1963. 167p.
Punto del Este. The limits of collective security in a troubled hemisphere . . . New York, 1962. 31p. (Carnegie Endowment for International Peace Occasional paper 3)

Rosenau, James N. Internal war as an international event (in his International, aspects of civil strife. Princeton, Princeton univ. press. 1964. pp.45—91)

Rosenau, James N., ed. International aspects of civil strife. Princeton, Princeton Univ. Press. 1964. 322p.

Ross, Alf. A textbook of international law. General part. London, New York, Longmans, Green. 1947. 313p.

154

Roth, Andreas H. Minimum standard of international law applied to aliens. Leyden, Sijthoff. 1949. 194p.

Satow, Sir Ernest M. A guide to diplomatic practice. 4th ed. edited by Nevile Bland. London, New York, Longmans, Green. 1957. 510p.

Scott, Andrew M. Internal violence as an instrument of cold warfare (in Rosenau, James N., ed. International aspects of civil strife. Princeton, Princeton univ. press, 1964, pp.154—69)

Shea, Donald R. The Calvo clause; a problem of inter-American and international law and diplomacy. Minneapolis, Univ. of Minnesota Press. 1955. 323p.

Slater, Jerome. A revaluation of collective security, the OAS in action. Columbus, Ohio State Univ. Press. 1965. 56p.

Smyrdadis, Bion. La intervención ante la corte internacional de justicia. Buenos Aires. 1954. 6p.

Stanger, Roland J., ed. Essays on intervention. Columbus, Ohio State Univ. Press. 1964. 125p.

Stoetzer, O. C. The Organization of American states; an introduction. New York, Praeger. 1965. 213p.

Stone, Julius. Aggression and world order; a critique of United Nations theories of aggression. Berkeley, Univ. of California Press. 1958. 226p.

Stowell, Ellery Cory.
Intervention in international law. Washington, J. Byrne & Co. 1921. 558p.
La théorie et la pratique de l'intervention. 1932. 40 Recueil des Cours 91—148.

Tansill, Charles Callan. The United States and Santo Domingo 1798—1873; a chapter in Caribbean diplomacy. Baltimore, Johns Hopkins Press. 1938. 487p.

Thomas, Ann Van Wynen and Thomas, A. J., jr.
Non-intervention; the law and its import in the Americas. Dallas, Southern Methodist Univ. Press. 1956. 476p.
The Organization of American states. Dallas, Southern Methodist Univ. Press. 1963. 530p.

Visscher, Charles de. Theory and reality in public international law. Princeton, Princeton Univ. Press. 1957. 381p.

Waldock, C. H. M. The regulation of the use of force by individual states in international law. 1952. 81 Recueil des Cours 455—514.

Washington Center of Foreign Policy Research. The future character and role of peace observation arrangements under the United Nations: cases under inter-American organizations and procedures. Washington. 1964. 340p.

Whiteman, Marjorie M. Digest of international law. Washington, Gov't Print. Off. 1963—65. 5v. (in progress) V.1, pp.321—702, Nonintervention.

Wilson, Larman C. The principle of nonintervention in inter-American relations. Doctoral dissertation in preparation, Univ. of Maryland.

PERIODICAL REFERENCES

General

√ Augelli, J. P. Dominican Republic (bibliography). May 1965. 15 Focus 1—6.

√ Berle, Adolf A., jr. A stitch in time. May 20, 1965. 32 Reporter 22—23.

√ Bosch, Juan.
Communism and democracy in the Dominican Republic. Aug. 7, 1965. 48 Saturday Review 13—15.
La crise dominicaine est une crise de la démocratie en Amérique. July/Aug. 1965. Croissance des Jeunes Nations 18—21.
Más cuentos escritos en el exilio. Santo Domingo, Librería Dominicana. 1964. 284p.
A tale of two nations: Dominican-American diplomacy. June 21, 1965. 48 New Leader 3—7.
Why I was overthrown: the Dominican debacle. Oct. 14, 1963. 46 New Leader 3—4.

Camargo, P. P. Human rights and democracy 1963. 15 (5) Américas 33—36.

Claude, Inis L., jr. The OAS, the UN and the United States. March 1964. Int'l Conciliation 1—67 .

Connell-Smith, Gordon.
The future of the Organization of American states—significance of the Punta del Este conference, March 1962. 18 World Today 112—20.
The Organization of American states. 1960. 16 World Today 447—56.
OAS and the Dominican crisis. 1965. 21 World Today 229—36.

√ Dodd, Thomas J. Vietnam and Latin America—the danger of a hemispheric Vietnam. Sept. 15, 1965. 31 Vital Speeches 706—9.

√ Dominican Republic. May 7, 1965. 23 Cong. Q. Weekly Rep. 873—74.

√ Draper, Theodore.
Bosch and communism: analyzing the charges. Oct. 14, 1963. 46 New Leader 9—14.
Dominican crisis: case study in American policy. Dec. 1965. 40 Commentary 33—38.

156

The roots of the Dominican crisis: words vs. deeds. May 24, 1965. 48 New Leader 3—18.

Dreier, John C.
The council of the OAS: performance and potential. 1963. 5 J. Inter-Am. Studies 297—312.
The Organization of American states and United States policy. 1963. 17 Int'l Org. 36—53.

Etzioni, A. Le succès et le déclin de la politique "d'intervention pour le progrès" en République dominicaine. 1965. 15 Civilisations 227—42.

Evans, Rowland, jr. First steps in Dominican democracy. Jan. 3, 1963. 28 Reporter 21—23.

Fleming, D. F. Can Pax Americana succeed? 1965. 360 Annals 127—38.

Fougerolle, Xavier de. République dominicaine—quarte années de crise. 1965. 21 Rev. de Défense Nationale 1236—46.

Geyelin, Philip.
Big obstacles confront U.S. efforts to forge a Dominican regime: factional hatreds, economic, social ills pose problems. May 28, 1965. 165 Wall St. J. 1—.
Dominican dilemma: extricating U.S. forces, preventing new "Cuba" may take long time. May 4, 1965. 165 Wall St. J. 1—.
Dominican impasse: Imbert tightens hold over island, but U.S., OAS now oppose him. Washington seeks compromise regime . . . June 2, 1965. 165 Wall St. J. 1—.
Dominican tremors: unrest in hemisphere rises: so does concern over subversion peril. May 25, 1965. 165 Wall St. J. 1—.
OAS idosyncrasies: Dominican crisis upsets lethargic Latin habits. May 11, 1965. 165 Wall St. J. 16.

Goldenberg, B. Die dominikanische tragödie—zur nordamerikanischen intervention in der Dominikanischen Republik im frühjahr 1965. 1965. 20 Europa-Archiv 521—28.

Halper, Sam. The Dominican upheaval: a revolution delayed. May 10, 1965. 48 New Leader 3—4.

Hennessy, A. Background to the Dominican coup. 1965. 21 World Today 236—39.

Manger, William. The Organization of American states: present problems and future prospects. 1962. 4 World Justice 5—13.

Martin, Andrew. Human rights and world politics. 1951. 5 Yb. World Aff. 37—80.

Martin, Paul. Peace-keeping and the United Nations. 1964. 40 Int'l Aff. 191—204.

Roche, John P. Return of the syndicate: epitaph for Dominican democracy. Oct. 14, 1963. 46 New Leader. 5—8.

✓ Smith, Robert Freeman.   Social revolution in Latin America. 1965.
41 Int'l Aff. 637—49.

✓Tannenbaum, Frank.   The United States and Latin America. June
1961. 76 Pol. Sci. Q. 161—80.

Wells, Henry.
The OAS and the Dominican elections.   1963. 7 Orbis 150—63.
Turmoil in the Dominican Republic.   1966. 50 Current Hist.
14—20.

✓ Wilson, L. C.   The Dominican policy of the United States. 1965.
128 World Aff. 93—101.

Wood, B. and Morales, M.   Latin America and the United Nations. 1965. 18 Int'l Org. 714—27.

✓ Wrights, Theodore P., jr.
Free elections in the Latin American policy of the United States.
1959. 74 Pol. Sci. Q. 89—112.
The United States and Latin American dictatorship: the case of
the Dominican Republic.   1960. J. Int'l Aff. (No.2) 152—57.

Legal

Accioly, Hildebrando.   O princípio de naointervencao e a con-
vencao de Havana sobre lutas civis. 1949. Inter-Am. Jurid. Yb.
3—8.

Andraos, Adly.   De l'intervention dans les affaires intérieures des
états souverains. 1954. 10 Rev. Egyptienne de Droit Int'l 1—23.

Arias, Harmodio.   The non-liability of states for damages suffered
by foreigners in the course of a riot, an insurrection or a civil
war. 1913. 7 Am. J. Int'l L. 724—66.

Ball, M. Margaret.   Issue for the Americas: non-intervention v.
human rights and the preservation of democratic institutions.
1961. 15 Int'l Org. 21—37.

Bartelle, Talmadge L.   Counterinsurgency and civil war. 1964. 40
N.D.L. Rev. 254—91.

Borchard, Edwin.   The "minimum standard" of the treatment of
aliens. 1939. 33 Am. Soc'y Int'l L. Proc. 51—74.

Brownlie, Ian.   The use of force in self-defence. 1961. 37 Brit. Yb.
Int'l L. 183—268.

Caicedo Castilla, J. J.   La Organización de los estados americanos.
1963. 22 Estudios de Derecho 7—22; 23 (401) Justicia 29—44.

Carey, John and Irving, J. Bruce.   The Dominican crisis: a case
study of law in action at the Security council. 1965. 9 A.B.A. Sec.
Int'l & Comp. L. Bull, 23—34.

The crisis in the Dominican Republic.   Dec. 1960. Int'l Comm'n
Jurists Bull. 23—27.

Diaz Doin, Guillermo.   La Organización de estados americanos

y la no intervencion. Mayo/Junio 1960. 110 (3) Cuadernos
Americanos 73—88.

Dupuy, R. J. Organisation internationale et unité politique—la
crise de l'organisation des états américains. 1960. 6 Ann. Francais
de Droit Int'l 185—224.

Falk, Richard A. The United States and the doctrine of nonintervention in the internal affairs of independent states. 1959. 5
How. L.J. 163—89.

Fenwick, Charles G.
The competence of the council of the Organization of American
states. 1949. Inter-Am. Jurid. Yb. 21—39.
The Dominican Republic: intervention and collective self-de-
fense. 1966. 60 Am. J. Int'l L. 64—67.
Inter-American regional procedures for the settlement of dis-
putes. 1956. 10 Int'l Org. 12—21.
Intervention and the inter-American rule of law. 1959. 53 Am.
J. Int'l L. 873—76.
Intervention: individual and collective. 1945. 39 Am. J. Int'l
L. 645—63.
The issues at Punta del Este: nonintervention v. collective se-
curity. 1962. 56 Am. J. Int'l 469—74.
The Organization of American states. 1965. 59 Am. J .Int'l L.
315—20.

Firmage, E. B. A United Nations peace force. 1965. 11 Wayne L.
Rev. 717—38.

Friedmann, Wolfgang. Intervention, civil war and the role of
international law. 1965. 59 Am. Soc'y Int'l L. Proc. 67—81.

Fuchs, Gilles. La commission interamericaine de la paix. 1957.
3 Ann. Francais de Droit Int'l 142—49.

Fulbright, J. William. The situation in the Dominican Republic
—compliance with the law. Oct. 1, 1965, 31 Vital Speeches
747—55.

Fundamental challenges to legal doctrines affecting international
coercion: aggression, self-defense, nonintervention, self-determination, neutrality (Panel discussion: Milton Katz, Louis Henkin,
Eli Whitney Debevoise, Myres S. McDougal, Charles M. Spof-
ford). 1963. 57 Am. J. Int'l L. Proc. 146—73.

Garcia-Mora, Manuel R.
International law and the law of hostile military expeditions.
1958. 27 Fordham L. Rev. 309—31.
The law of the inter-American treaty of reciprocal assistance.
1951. 20 Fordham L. Rev. 1—22.

Gardner, Richard N. The development of the peace-keeping capacity of the United Nations. 1963. 57 Am. Soc'y Int'l L. Proc. 224—38.

Godoy, Horacio H. International law and the new movement in Latin America. 1960. 54 Am. Soc'y Int'l L. Proc. 96—101.

Goebel, Julius. The international responsibility of states for injuries sustained by aliens on account of mob violence, insurrections and civil wars. 1914. 8 Am. J. Int'l L. 802—52.

Graber, Doris Appel. United States intervention in Latin America. 1962. 16 Yb. World Aff. 23—50.

Halderman, John W. Regional enforcement measures and the United Nations. 1963. 52 Geo. L.J. 89—118.

Henkin, Louis. Force, intervention and neutrality in contemporary international law. 1963. 57 Am. Soc'y Int'l L. Proc. 145—73.

Higgins, Rosalyn. The legal limits to the use of force by sovereign state. United Nations practice. 1961. 37 Brit. Yb. Int'l L. 269—319.

L'Huillier, J. Intervention et non-intervention dans la charte des Nations unies. 1951. 4 Rev. Hellénique de Droit Int'l 253—60.

Human rights; investigations of execution of political prisoners. Aug. 1965. 17 Américas 40—41.

Inter-American draft convention on human rights. 1962. 4 J. Int'l Comm'n Jurists 160—84.

Irizarry y Puente, J. The doctrines of recognition and intervention in Latin America. 1954. 28 Tul. L. Rev. 313—42.

Komarnicki, Titus. L'intervention en droit international moderne. 1956. 60 Rev. Générlae de Droit Int'l Pub. 521—68.

Kunz, Josef L. Individual and collective self-defense in article 51 of the charter of the United Nations. 1947. 41/Am. J. Int'l L. 872—79.

Lacarte, Julio A. The Latin American system. 1959. 53 Am. Soc'y Int'l L. Proc. 62—68.

Lador-Lederer, J. J.
Intervention a historical stocktaking. 1959. 29 Nordisk Tidsshrift für Int'l Recht 127.
Zenith and decay of the doctrine of non-intervention of states in the internal affairs of other states. Aug. 1958. 5 (11) Congrès Int'l de Droit Comparé, Rapports Généraux 921.

Lerche, Charles O., jr. Development of rules relating to peacekeeping by the Organization of American states. 1965. 59 Am. Soc'y Int'l L. Proc. 60—66.

MacChesney, Brunson. International protection of human rights in the United Nations. 1952. 47 Nw. U. L. Rev. 198—222.

McDougal, Myres S. and Bebr, Gerhard. Human rights in the United Nations. 1964. 58 Am. J. Int'l L. 603—41.

160

Madrazzo, J. A. Intervención (en derecho internacional). 1962. 16 Enciclopedio Jurídica Omeba 671—82.

Millington, Thomas M. U.S. diplomacy and the Dominican crisis. Summer 1963. 7 School of Advanced Int'l Studies Rev. 25—30.

Mora, José A.
The Organization of American states. 1960. 14 Int'l Org. 514—23.
The role of the Organization of American states. 1961. 16 Record 263—70.

Morrison, De Lesseps S. The U.S. and the O.A.S. April 1963. 2 Yale Pol. 17.

Murdock, James Oliver. Collective security distinguished from intervention. 1962. 56 Am. J. Int'l L. 500—03.

Murdock, James Oliver and Gobbi, Hugo J. The inter-American juridical committee. 1960. 9 Am. J. Comp. L. 596—605.

O'Brien, W. V. International law, morality and American intervention. Sept. 1965. 201 Catholic World 288—93.

Plank, John N. The Caribbean: intervention, when and how. 1965. 44 For. Aff. 37—48.

Rendón, G. García. L'Organisation des republiques américaines et le maintien de la paix. Bruxelles, Le Droit au Service de la Paix (Dec. 1957, no.2)

Romero Carranza, Ambrosio. Excepciones legítimas y legales al principio de no intervencion. Sept./Oct. 1961. Juris. Argentina. (1961—V—sec. doc. pp.39—45)

Ronning, C. Neale. Intervention, international law and the inter-American system. 1961. 3 J. Inter-Am. Studies 249—71.

Rougier, Antoine. Le théorie de intervention d'humanité. 1910. 17 Rev. Génerale de Droit Int'l Pub. 468—526.

Russell, Ruth B. Development by the United Nations of rules relating to peacekeeping. 1965. 59 Am. Soc'y Int'l L. Proc. 53—60.

Sandifer, Durward V. Human rights in the inter-American system. 1965. 11 How. L.J. 508—26.

Schacht Aristequieta, E. Auto-determinación e intervención. 1962. 25 Rev. del Colegio de Abogados del Distrito Federal 97—108.

Schachter, Oscar. The uses of law in international peacekeeping. 1964. 50 Va. L. Rev. 1096—1114.

Scheman, L. R. The Inter-American commission on human rights. 1965. 59 Am. J. Int'l L. 335—43.

Sepulveda, C. The inter-American system: some modest proposals for change. 1965. 1 J. U. Texas Int'l Soc'y 15—33.

✓ Slater, J. The United States, the Organization of American states and the Dominican Republic, 1961—63. 1964. 18 Int'l Org. 268—91.

161

Sohn, Louis B. The role of the United Nations in civil wars. 1963. 57 Am. Soc'y Int'l L. Proc. 208—15.

Thomas, A. J., jr.
Non-intervention and public order in the Americas. 1959. 53 Am. Soc'y Int'l L. Proc. 72—80.
The Organization of American states and subversive intervention. 1961 55 Am. Soc'y Int'l L. Proc. 19—24.

Thomas, A. J., jr. and Thomas, A. V. W. Democracy and the Organization of American states. 1961. 46 Minn. L. Rev. 337—82.

Travis, Martin B., jr. The political and social bases for the Latin American doctrine of non-intervention. 1959. 53 Am. Soc'y Int'l Proc. 68—72.

Vasquez Carrizosa, Alfredo. La crisis del derecho americano. 1962. 2 (7) Foro Internacional 423—39.

Wells, Henry. The OAS and the Dominican elections. Spring 1963. Orbis 150—63.

Winfield, P. H.
The grounds of intervention in international law. 1924. 5 Brit. Yb. Int'l L. 147—62.
The history of intervention in international law. 1922/23. 3 Brit. Yb. Int'l L. 130—49.

PERTINENT ARTICLES OF THE
UNITED NATIONS CHARTER

Article 33

1. The parties to any dispute, the continuance of which is likely to endanger the maintenance of international peace and security, shall, first of all, seek a solution by negotiation, enquiry, mediation, conciliation, arbitration, judicial settlement, resort to regional agencies or arrangements, or other peaceful means of their own choice.

2. The Security Council shall, when it deems necessary, call upon the parties to settle their dispute by such means.

Article 34

The Security Council may investigate any dispute, or any situation which might lead to international friction or give rise to a dispute, in order to determine whether the continuance of the dispute or situation is likely to endanger the maintenance of international peace and security.

Article 35

1. Any Member of the United Nations may bring any dispute, or any situation of the nature referred to in Article 34, to the attention of the Security Council or of the General Assembly.

2. A state which is not a Member of the United Nations may bring to the attention of the Security Council or of the General Assembly any dispute to which it is a party if it accepts in advance, for the purposes of the dispute, the obligations of pacific settlement provided in the present Charter.

3. The proceedings of the General Assembly in respect of matters brought to its attentation under, this Article will be subject to the provisions of Articles 11 and 12.

Article 51

Nothing in the present Charter shall impair the inherent right of individual or collective self-defense if an armed attack occurs against a Member of the United Nations, until the Security Council has taken measures necessary to maintain international peace and security. Measures taken by Members in the exercise of this right of self-defense shall be immediately reported to the Security Council and shall not in any way affect the authority and responsibility of the Security Council under the present Charter to take at any time such action as it deems necessary in order to maintain or restore international peace and security.

Article 52

1. Nothing in the present Charter precludes the existence of regional arrangements or agencies for dealing with such matters relating to the maintenance of international peace and security as are appropriate for regional action, provided that such arrangements or agencies and their activities are consistent with the Purposes and Principles of the United Nations.

2. The Members of the United Nations entering into such arrangements or constituting such agencies shall make every effort to achieve pacific settlement of local disputes through such regional arrangements or by such regional agencies before referring them to the Security Council.

3. The Security Council shall encourage the development of pacific settlement of local disputes through such regional arrangements or by such regional agencies either on the initiative of the states concerned or by reference from the Security Council.

4. This Article in no way impairs the application of Articles 34 and 35.

Article 54

The Security Council shall at all times be kept fully informed of activities undertaken or in contemplation under regional arrangements or by regional agencies for the maintenance of international peace and security.